We're So Blessed

We're So Blessed

Forty Days of Devotions
and Activities for the
WHOLE FAMILY

Taylor, Madison, and Logan Cain
With Jared Johnson

BOOKS

We're So Blessed: Forty Days of Devotions and Activities for the Whole Family

Published by KLOVE Books, a partner of Forefront Books.
Distributed by Simon & Schuster.

Library of Congress Control Number: 2024923158

Print ISBN: 978-1-63763-360-1
E-book ISBN: 978-1-63763-361-8

Cover Design by Bruce Gore, Gore Studio, Inc.
Interior Design by Bill Kersey, KerseyGraphics

Printed in the United States of America

For Beau: Our memories of you will keep us feeling so blessed until we see you again in heaven. We love and miss you, sweet boy.

Contents

Introduction

If you could have been a fly on the wall in our quaint childhood home in small-town Alabama, you would have witnessed the beautiful chaos in which we Cain siblings grew up. You would have seen the eldest (*and best*) of us, Taylor, skillfully plucking her acoustic guitar and figuring out all the harmony parts to a Steven Curtis Chapman song. You would have seen the middle sibling and glue of the family, Madison, playing with the family video camera while acting out a homemade skit. And you would have seen baby brother, Logan, doing just about anything to get under the skin of his two older sisters. Our childhood was full of wild memories, great laughter, and light. And every bit of that is due to our intentional, loving parents and pastors, Charley and Shari Cain.

Even in the craziness of a home with three children all separated by one year in age, our mom and dad poured their all into each day. They supported our wildest dreams, they worked alongside us on last-minute school projects, and they created core memories for us we will never forget. We were the direct beneficiaries of God-centered family time, and now—as we've grown older, gotten married, and have had children of our own—we feel the challenge of establishing God as the head of our own homes.

We feel the challenge of quieting the discord of this world and creating a home for our children to grow not only in stature but in spirit and in truth. We want to cultivate the same deep connections with our growing families that our parents so thoughtfully cultivated with us. That challenge led us to the creation of this family devotional. Our prayer is that through these daily readings both our own families and yours can glean from God's Word together, notice the blessings of God together, and experience memorable moments and conversations *together*.

We're So Blessed is a forty-day, family-oriented devotional to help guide you and your family away from the madness of the world to a place of peace with God. It is an aid to help your family take the time to recognize God's hand in your everyday lives and to realize how truly blessed you are as children of God. This devotional is designed to be enjoyed *together,* and it is written in a way that is attainable and meaningful for all members of the family. Each day of the devotional is composed of three elements:

1. Approachable passages from God's Word
2. Relatable, personal stories from the entire Cain family, our spouses, and our children
3. Meaningful family conversation starters and activities to do as a family

Through each day's reading, we pray that your family feels encouraged by God's Word, you feel *seen* relating to our zany stories, and your family feels inspired to create some unforgettable moments of your own. You can gather around the kitchen table or the living room couch, open this devotional, and let it serve as the launchpad for Spirit-filled conversations and laughter-filled activities that leave your family feeling refreshed, refocused, and reminded that *We're So Blessed.*

Lost & Found

Scripture

Parable of the Lost Sheep • Matthew 18:12–14

[12] *"If a man has a hundred sheep and one of them wanders away, what will he do? Won't he leave the ninety-nine others on the hills and go out to search for the one that is lost?* [13] *And if he finds it, I tell you the truth, he will rejoice over it more than over the ninety-nine that didn't wander away!* [14] *In the same way, it is not my heavenly Father's will that even one of these little ones should perish."*

Madison's Hide & Seek (Taylor)

Growing up, Madison wasn't what you would call a "bad kid"; she was just "curious." Sometimes she might have been a little *too* curious. After one particular day of playing with family friends, Madison wasn't quite ready for the fun to be finished. She hoped to spend the night with our friends and keep the good times rolling, but to her disappointment, our parents said, "No, not tonight." But even though she heard "no," Madison's mind began to come up with a plan. She thought to herself, *If I can just hide in the back of our friends' car, they will drive all the way back home and then I can pop out for a big "Surprise!"*

moment. We'll all laugh, and they'll be so happy that I'll be able spend the night after all.

So, without telling a soul, Madison quietly opened the minivan door, crawled like a worm until she was hidden under the back seat, and stayed as quiet as a mouse. Before too long, our family friends loaded into their minivan, cranked the engine, and began the long drive back home. Madison had done it! She had successfully hidden and was now along for the ride. Now she just had to wait for the right moment to pop out and give everyone the biggest surprise of their lives!

Meanwhile, it wasn't long before Mom and Dad realized they hadn't seen Madison in a while. They checked in her bedroom, they checked in the living room, they checked the backyard...no Madison. They checked with the neighbors, and Madison wasn't there either, so panic began to set in. Our parents loaded into our old minivan and drove through the neighborhood searching high and low for Madison. When they couldn't find her, they began calling friends to help with their search. They even got the local police department involved, and a full hunt for Madison ensued. With terror in their minds, our parents sped down the highway and eventually caught up to our family friends and waved them over to the side of the road. Little did they know, a very well-hidden Madison lay quietly giggling under the back seat.

"Have you seen Madison?" Dad shouted worriedly. "We haven't seen her since you all left the house. We're getting worried, and we've already called the police!"

"No, we haven't seen her!" they replied.

Finally, to Madison, the moment she was waiting for had come. She wriggled out from under the back seat, jumped up into the air, and shouted "Surprise!" But to *her* surprise, the look on everyone's faces wasn't pure happiness. They all nearly fainted with relief as their worst nightmare was resolved: Madison was not lost but found.

Mom and Dad wanted to be angry, but in that moment, they couldn't feel anything but pure joy and relief to see sweet Madison's smiling face again. Dad scooped Madison into his arms and carried her home more thankful than ever to have his "curious" daughter back in his sight. Just like our Dad stopping at nothing to find Madison, our God loves us so much that He will find us when we *too* are lost and far from Him and bring us home safe to His presence. Today's scripture tells us that it is not God's will that we should perish, but He desires to bring us "home" to a relationship with Him. And when we are back at home with our God, as verse 13 says, *"He will rejoice."*

Reflection Questions

- *What part of the Parable of the Lost Sheep stands out to you?*
- *What do you think of the shepherd leaving his ninety-nine other sheep to find the lost one?*
- *Does Madison's dad react like the shepherd when Madison goes missing?*
- *God loves us so much that He will come and find us when we're lost and bring us home safe. How does that make you feel?*

Activity

It's time for a good old-fashioned game of sardines! Choose one family member to go hide, and then everyone else looks for them. If you find the person hiding, you have to hide with them! The last person to find the hiders is "it" and hides first next round. Happy hiding!

....
....
....
....
....
....
....
....
....
....
....
....
....
....
....
....

Sneaking in Joy

Scripture

Living as Those Made Alive in Christ • Colossians 3:1–4, 12–17 ESV

[1] *If then you have been raised with Christ, seek the things that are above, where Christ is, seated at the right hand of God.* [2] *Set your minds on things that are above, not on things that are on earth.* [3] *For you have died, and your life is hidden with Christ in God.* [4] *When Christ who is your life appears, then you also will appear with Him in glory* ... [12] *Put on then, as God's chosen ones, holy and beloved, compassionate hearts, kindness, humility, meekness, and patience,* [13] *bearing with one another and, if one has a complaint against another, forgiving each other; as the Lord has forgiven you, so you also must forgive.* [14] *And above all these put on love, which binds everything together in perfect harmony.* [15] *And let the peace of Christ rule in your hearts, to which indeed you were called in one body. And be thankful.* [16] *Let the word of Christ dwell in you richly, teaching and admonishing one another in all wisdom, singing psalms and hymns and spiritual songs, with thankfulness in your hearts to God.* [17] *And whatever you do, in word or deed, do everything in the name of the Lord Jesus, giving thanks to God the Father through him.*

Taylor's Secret Visitor (Madison)

In 2015, when Taylor was 26 years old, she went on a mission trip to Honduras. Taylor loved this experience; she played with the local children, sang songs, and helped work on some building projects in the community. However, after she returned home, Taylor found herself very sick. After several days of sickness and no relief in sight, we took her to the hospital. What the doctors discovered was much worse than Taylor and our family had hoped. Her kidneys were in such critical shape that she might have to take powerful medicine for the rest of her life, and she might experience changes that would really break her heart, such as losing her ability to sing.

Taylor had to stay in the hospital for several days, and to help keep her company, our whole family stayed with her. There in her tiny hospital room, we crammed air mattresses and blankets and tried our best to not trip over one another. It was crowded and uncomfortable, and each day brought more frightening news about Taylor's sickness. However, we all made it a point that no matter the discomfort we experienced lying on the floor or the fear we felt in our hearts for Taylor, we would choose to stay positive and believe that God would heal Taylor's kidneys. We did everything we could do to "let the peace of God rule in our hearts," as the scripture above says. We did this by playing games, watching funny movies, telling jokes, and singing songs. We all prayed together and sang praise and worship songs to God throughout the day. When we felt scared, we chose to focus on Jesus and not on all the bad news around us.

Then when the bad news seemed to be at its worst, Logan and I came up with a big idea to help encourage Taylor. We wanted to bring her a special visitor to cheer her up ... our family dog, Pepe. However, dogs weren't allowed in the hospital, so we had to be very careful. We went home, gathered up Pepe, the largest suitcase we owned (it helped that Pepe was on the smaller side), and all the dog treats we could carry, and headed back to the hospital. Then we carefully placed Pepe into the suitcase along with several of his favorite treats, and Pepe began to happily chow down as we carried him secretly to Taylor's hospital room.

We walked into the hospital room, placed the suitcase on Taylor's bed, unzipped it—and out popped Pepe! Taylor was so happy to pet her dog and have a sense of "home" even at the hospital. In that moment, Taylor wasn't thinking about being sick, she was thinking about how thankful she was for Jesus and her family. She smiled and hugged Pepe all night long.

Finally, after many scary days, Taylor got the report that she had been longing for: she was healed and could go home! Her sickness miraculously improved and she was able to make a full recovery. Taylor and our family praised God and celebrated the mighty work He had done. All along the way we tried to "be thankful," "sing hymns with thankfulness in our hearts," and "let the peace of God rule," and it helped bring us closer together even in a trying time. Most importantly, when we were most afraid, we "put on love" by encouraging and caring for one another. Sometimes putting on love means playing games together, sometimes it means praying together when times are tough, and sometimes it means sneaking joy (in the form of a dog) into a hospital!

Reflection Questions

- *How can you "sneak joy" into your family?*

- *What is something nice someone in your family has done to encourage you?*
- *What is your favorite way to give thanks to God?*

Activity

It's praising time! Find your family's favorite praise and worship song and crank it up! Sing together and thank God for all the good things He has done for your family. Bonus points if you even add in some dance moves!

....

....

....

....

....

....

....

....

....

....

....

....

....

....

Staying Prepared

Scripture

Parable of the Ten Bridesmaids • Matthew 25:1-13

[1]*"Then the Kingdom of Heaven will be like ten bridesmaids who took their lamps and went to meet the bridegroom.* [2] *Five of them were foolish, and five were wise.* [3] *The five who were foolish didn't take enough olive oil for their lamps,* [4] *but the other five were wise enough to take along extra oil.* [5] *When the bridegroom was delayed, they all became drowsy and fell asleep.* [6] *At midnight they were roused by the shout, 'Look, the bridegroom is coming! Come out and meet him!'* [7] *All the bridesmaids got up and prepared their lamps.* [8] *Then the five foolish ones asked the others, 'Please give us some of your oil because our lamps are going out.'* [9] *But the others replied, 'We don't have enough for all of us. Go to a shop and buy some for yourselves.'* [10] *But while they were gone to buy oil, the bridegroom came. Then those who were ready went in with him to the marriage feast, and the door was locked.* [11] *Later, when the other five bridesmaids returned, they stood outside, calling, 'Lord! Lord! Open the door for us!'* [12] *But he called back, 'Believe me, I don't know you!'* [13] *So you, too, must keep watch! For you do not know the day or hour of my return."*

Charley's Chocolate Syrup (Logan)

There is a well-known fact in the Cain family. If the patriarch, Pastor Charley Cain, is going to the grocery store for *anything* at all—whether it be a loaf of bread or a jug of laundry detergent—he's coming home with one extra item . . . chocolate syrup. It's an easy item to forget. It typically sits in the crowded condiments shelf in the Cain family refrigerator, and it isn't used every day, or every week for that matter. So each time Pastor Charley goes to the grocery store, the thought occurs to him, *Do we have any chocolate syrup at the house?* Before you know it, the Cain family has three or four bottles of syrup tucked safely away in their refrigerator.

And while it seems just like a funny case of forgetfulness, the heart behind it is anything but forgetful. Pastor Charley knows that nothing brings his family together like enjoying a sweet treat. Every time the family is all in one place, no matter how large of a dinner we just enjoyed, there always seems to be room for everyone to enjoy a bowl of ice cream with chocolate syrup. It's these moments together where the family laughs, dreams, and shares the truest parts of themselves with one another. Through perfect, syrupy bites, family achievements are celebrated and family losses are comforted. Nothing binds a family quite like ice cream.

Each time Pastor Charley picks up yet *another* bottle of chocolate syrup, ultimately, he's being obedient to his calling as the spiritual head of his household. He's making an investment in his family, an investment in what will be a future moment shared with his children and grandchildren. Like the five wise bridesmaids waiting on the bridegroom with ample oil, Charley prepares himself and his home to host a meaningful time with all of us—no matter *when* that time may come. As the years have passed, these moments together may not be as frequent as they once were, but they are more valuable than ever. Each time these family moments occur, you can guarantee that there will be chocolate syrup for everyone's ice cream.

Reflection Questions

- *What was the significance of the bridesmaids preparing oil for their lamps? What happened to those who hadn't prepared enough oil?*
- *The oil in the bridesmaids' lamps signified obedience to God. What are some ways you can store up "oil" in your life to help you stay close to God?*
- *In the same way Charley invested in his family by making preparations for a family ice cream night, what is a way you can invest in your family to create meaningful moments together?*

Activity

You guessed it: time for a family ice cream party! Someone grab the bowls, spoons, and ice cream of your choice; someone grab all the toppings (especially the chocolate syrup); and everyone make their favorite ice cream sundae. Turn off the TV, put away the phones and screens, and enjoy some ice cream and conversation together!

A Curious Mind

Scripture

Unity in the Body • Ephesians 4:2-3

[2] *Always be humble and gentle. Be patient with each other, making allowance for each other's faults because of your love.*
[3] *Make every effort to keep yourselves united in the Spirit, binding yourselves together with peace.*

Madison's Blue Phase (Taylor)

As a child Madison was certainly a well-mannered young girl. She minded our parents, was respectful to others, and played kindly with any kid she'd meet. However, as mannerly as she was, her curious mind would get her into a little trouble from time to time. Our parents now say with a chuckle that if Madison was ever quiet you needed to find her *quickly*! She was just so curious about the world around her, and sometimes that curiosity led her to innocently do some rather mischievous things.

When Madison was five years old, while our parents were merely one room away, her curiosity led her to the family's "junk" drawer in the kitchen. This drawer was a catch-all for rubber bands, paper clips, pencils, and, on this fateful day, an extra-large, dark blue permanent marker.

Madison was mesmerized by the marker. She removed the cap to reveal the dark blue tip, and that's when her curious mind took over. Madison thought, *Wow, with a big marker like this, I bet I could color my entire leg blue.* That thought was very quickly put into action. Calmly and quietly, young Madison applied deep blue marker strokes to her leg. She meticulously colored in heavy ink, solid line by solid line, until, lo and behold, her entire leg looked just like a blueberry. Madison sat back, astonished with her masterpiece. Again, she thought to herself, *This looks amazing. I can't wait to show Mom and Dad. They'll be so impressed!*

Madison walked gingerly into the living room where our parents were sitting, and when she had her blue leg displayed proudly, she shouted "Surprise!" And it was *indeed* a surprise. Our parents shared dumbfounded looks as they figured out what exactly they were witnessing. Then they frantically delivered a bevy of questions: "What have you done? Which marker did you use? Did you know this was a *permanent* marker?" Madison beamed with pride as she truthfully answered each question: "I colored my leg! I used the big marker in the junk drawer…and no I didn't realize it was permanent." Mom and Dad quickly took her into the bathroom and began desperately trying to wash away the blue ink with soap and water. While a slight amount was removed, it was evident after the fourth or fifth wash that this blue leg was here to stay until it could gradually fade over time. And until it faded, it would be quite the conversation piece for our parents around town.

Madison wasn't a bad kid in the slightest; she was just whole-heartedly curious. And in this situation, like many others, our parents decided to respond with patience and gentleness. While they explained that applying homemade, permanent marker tattoos *wasn't* a great idea, they also were careful not to dissuade Madison from inquiring about the world around her. They had the foresight to know that a curious child like her would grow into an intelligent, inquisitive adult. As today's scriptures instruct, they were patient with her and made allowances for her faults and missteps because of their love for her as they raised her into a strong, confident woman of faith.

Reflection Questions

- *Has curiosity ever gotten you into trouble? If so, share that story with your family.*
- *Ephesians 4:2 says to make allowances for one another's faults because of your love. How can you live out that scripture? How can you make better allowances for others?*
- *Think of a time someone was patient with you. How did that make you feel?*

Activity

Now for a less permanent version of Madison's Blue Phase: it's washable marker tattoo time! All you'll need is a box of washable markers and each other to use as a canvas. Take turns making wacky tattoos on one another. Be sure to take some photos to remember your artwork before you clean it off.

Love What You Have

Scripture

Freedom from Rules and New Life in Christ • Colossians 2:6–7

[6] *And now, just as you accepted Christ Jesus as your Lord, you must continue to follow him.* [7] *Let your roots grow down into him, and let your lives be built on him. Then your faith will grow strong in the truth you were taught, and you will overflow with thankfulness.*

Taylor's Treasure Map (Logan)

Growing up in the Cain household was anything but dull. With three young children all close in age, the house was always teeming with laughter and full of raucous games. However, on a particularly dreary day, we found ourselves stuck inside. All the games had been played, all the movies had been watched, and young Taylor and Madison found themselves to be surprisingly quite bored! Toys and books surrounded them on all sides, but the two of them just couldn't think of anything *new* to play. As they stared blankly out the living room window, Taylor, the typical leader of the Cain kid crew, devised a plan.

Their old, familiar toys had lost a bit of their luster, but Taylor thought to herself, *What if we could play with our old toys in a* new *way?* Without any explanation, Taylor quietly exited the room. She grabbed Madison's toy jewelry, which was once used for fun dress-up games but now sat lonely on the floor. Then she picked up a piece of paper and a pen and sneaked silently outside. The idea was simple: Taylor would take the toy jewelry to a remote location within our yard and bury it discreetly. Then, using the paper and pen, she would create a precise treasure map leading directly to the newly buried treasure. Now all she needed was a willing pirate to take part in the search.

Taylor ran inside with wide eyes. "Madison, you have to help! I found this treasure map, and it looks like it leads to something!" Madison's sense of boredom instantly left her body as she matched Taylor's excited energy. The search was on! Madison held the map tightly as she zigged and zagged all throughout the yard, following the directions on the map perfectly until . . . eureka! Madison had found the supposed treasure location and began to feverishly dig into the earth with her bare hands. Her digging proved successful as she unearthed her own toy jewelry with her smile a mile wide! She squealed with delight and clung to the toy jewelry like it was her most prized possession—so thankful to have successfully found this old, familiar toy. Thanks to Taylor's creativity, the same toy jewelry that had seemed worn out moments earlier was now Madison's most valuable treasure. Taylor could have given up on this day and succumbed to boredom, but she chose to rediscover the love for something she already had on hand. Ultimately, she realized the real treasure all along was creating a fun memory that she and Madison would cherish forever.

Much like a beloved toy we've taken for granted, we can often lose our sense of love and wonder for the ultimate gift of Jesus as our Lord. We initially accept Jesus' love and unmerited grace for us with such delight and gratefulness, but as the difficulties and repeated rhythms of life set in, our delight and gratefulness can sadly decline. Scripture challenges us to reverse this decline and grow our faith by letting our roots grow down deep into Him and building our lives on Him. When we choose to organize our lives around Jesus, we will continually rediscover our love for Him and our thankfulness for His presence.

Reflection Questions

- *When we first accept Jesus as our Lord, we often do so with excitement and thankfulness. But as we experience life and its struggles, this sense of excitement and thankfulness can start to wither. What does today's passage say we can do to combat this from happening?*

- *When we continue with Jesus and let our lives be built on Him, the scripture says our faith will grow and we will overflow with thankfulness. How have you noticed your faith growing? What are some specific elements in your life for which you are thankful?*

- *What is a practical way that you could reinvigorate your faith?*

Activity

It's time to take a page out of young Taylor's book. One person gets to be the hider and everyone else is a seeker. The hider takes a familiar household item and hides it secretly in the house (or you can even bury it in the yard with your parents' permission). Then the hider creates a map that will lead the seekers to the hidden treasure. See how long it takes for the seekers to find the hidden item!

....
....
....
....
....
....
....
....
....
....
....
....
....
....

Training Up Children

Scripture

Proverbs 22:6 ESV

⁶ *Train up a child in the way he should go; even when he is old he will not depart from it.*

Ablaze in a Manger (Taylor)

Christmastime traditions at the Cain house are not taken lightly. Each year during the holidays, several traditions are family staples: Christmas cookie baking, completing a Christmas-themed puzzle, watching countless classic Christmas movies, and reading the Christmas story from the Gospel of Luke. When we were younger, however, there was another major tradition: the reenactment of the birth of Jesus. Our whole family would participate to make it come to life. Mom would help create bedsheet shepherd costumes for me (Taylor) and Madison. She would even help make our younger brother, Logan, a simple costume so he could play various animals that were present in the manger. Dad would help narrate the scene and lead us in singing a Christmas carol while strumming his acoustic guitar.

During the 1996 Christmas season, the reenactment was perfectly set up. Mom had us girls dressed and ready to be two rather impressive shepherds, and she had Logan ready to execute his role as the manger's donkey. Small nativity scene figurines and candles were positioned on the living room coffee table as the centerpiece for this production. With the actors ready, Dad began to softly strum his guitar and lead the family in singing "Silent Night." The beginning of the song was the cue for the two child shepherds and donkey to make their way toward the nativity scene.

The music filled the living room and the spirit of Christmas was alive and well . . . until our manger donkey stumbled and bumped the coffee table. This slight misstep wouldn't have been a problem if there hadn't been lit candles placed all along the coffee table for dramatic effect. As the table shook, a mental image of toppling, lit candles flashed before Dad's eyes. He couldn't help but experience the instant fear that these candles could catch fire to our shepherd costumes, along with everything else in the living room. With catlike reflexes, Dad dropped his guitar and steadied both Logan and the shaking coffee table. Thankfully the wobbling candles settled before setting the living room nativity scene ablaze, and everyone let out a major sigh of relief.

Dad and Mom wanted to create a perfect and meaningful Christmas tradition with us, and they nearly had the living room go up in flames. They'd planned everything perfectly, but some-times even perfectly planned ideas have unexpected outcomes! However, even with the near fire and unsuccessful reenactment, our parents were very much successful in raising us to have both a love for the true meaning of Christmas and a love for spending time together as a family. Even into adulthood, we haven't departed from these traditions. We all still, with our own children in tow, race home to Hartselle, Alabama, each Christmas to celebrate the birth of Jesus and enjoy precious traditions together.

Reflection Questions

- *Do you have any family traditions? If so, what is everyone's favorite?*
- *Today's scripture instructs us to raise up a child in the ways of God and then, when they're no longer a child, they'll remain on that path. Parents, what is something you were raised to do as a child that you still do today as an adult?*
- *What is something you as a parent wish to train your children up on that they'll keep with them for life?*

Activity

Create a new family tradition together! It can be simple like a monthly popcorn and movie night, or elaborate like a family talent show—get creative, have fun with it, and put it on the calendar! The purpose is to create something fun and repeatable that your whole family can look forward to doing together for years to come.

....

....

....

....

....

....

Go the Extra Mile

Scripture

Matthew 5:38–42

[38] *"You have heard the law that says the punishment must match the injury: 'An eye for an eye, and a tooth for a tooth.'* [39] *But I say, do not resist an evil person! If someone slaps you on the right cheek, offer the other cheek also.* [40] *If you are sued in court and your shirt is taken from you, give your coat, too.* [41] *If a soldier demands that you carry his gear for a mile, carry it two miles.* [42] *Give to those who ask, and don't turn away from those who want to borrow."*

The Great Cowboy Hat Rescue (Taylor)

When Logan was a young boy, his most prized possession was a simple, brown felt cowboy hat. This hat was a fixture on Logan's head *every* day. If you ever saw Logan, you saw him in this beloved cowboy hat. It went as far as Logan sleeping in the hat too! Being that it was a child's dress-up hat, it wasn't made for this level of everyday wear. From time to time, the hat would get crumpled or torn, and each time, our dad would come to the rescue to straighten it out, sew up any tears, and have it looking good as new. It made Dad so happy each time to watch Logan skip away with his repaired cowboy hat sitting playfully on his head. But one fateful day, the treasured cowboy hat was nearly no more.

During a family retreat at a local lake, Logan was playing joyfully with some other children down by the water with his famous cowboy hat sitting proudly on his head. Then disaster struck! A stiff breeze rolled in, scooped the cowboy hat off Logan's head, and sent the hat barreling into the lake. Before Logan could grab his hat, it had already drifted far away from the shore. Logan feared his most favorite possession was lost forever, and he ran to our parents with tears in his eyes. All hope seemed lost, until Dad looked out over the lake, and, to his surprise, he could still make out a small, brown object floating along the surface of the lake—*the hat*! He sprung to action and ran down to the water. By this time the hat had drifted to the center of the lake, making a swimming recovery rather far and treacherous, but in true divine fashion, Dad scanned along the banks before his eyes fell on a lone, abandoned canoe. The vessel was small and well-worn, but for his dear son's beloved cowboy hat, Dad was willing to take a risk.

He climbed into the canoe, pushed away from the shore, and set sail toward the cowboy hat. After several minutes of tireless rowing, he secured the hat with an oar and dragged it into the canoe. The cowboy hat was saved! Once back on shore, our dad, tired but thankful, shook the water off of the cowboy hat and made his way to little Logan. Dad had visualized this moment on his long journey to the shore. *Logan will be so excited to see his hat! I'm sure he's going to jump for joy as soon as he sees what I've done for him.* Then the moment Dad had waited for: he crouched down and proudly presented the cowboy hat to Logan; his heart was full of anticipation. Logan turned, grabbed the hat, pressed it firmly onto his head and said, "Thanks." Our brother then bounded away to return to his friends down by the lake.

"Thanks" was not exactly the heartwarming reaction Dad had anticipated. He had risked life and limb to rescue this simple cowboy hat that he could have easily replaced at a local toy store. He'd sprung into action when everyone else was content to let the hat be lost forever. But Dad couldn't help but smile and laugh at Logan's reaction. He saved the hat not for the thanks and not for the response. Dad saved the hat because what mattered to his son, mattered to him. As today's scripture challenges, he went the extra mile for Logan for no other reason than because he deeply loved him . . . and he deeply loved Logan because he was *first* deeply loved by his Savior.

Reflection Questions

- *Have you ever done something nice for someone and their response was less than expected? How did that make you feel?*
- *Jesus' words in the scripture above challenge us to love those who are unthankful, those who hurt us. What is a practical way you can put this verse into action in your life?*

Activity

As a family, sit down and think of a way that all of you can bless someone else. Whether that be giving them a gift, sending an encouraging card, or providing an act of service, think of the person and make your plan to give to them freely, without expecting anything in return. Happy giving!

A Father's Love

Scripture

Matthew 7:9–11

[9]*"You parents—if your children ask for a loaf of bread, do you give them a stone instead?* [10] *Or if they ask for a fish, do you give them a snake? Of course not!* [11] *So if you sinful people know how to give good gifts to your children, how much more will your heavenly Father give good gifts to those who ask him."*

Home Run Race (Madison)

It was a steamy Alabama night at the local baseball diamond, and twelve-year-old Logan was up to bat. The powerful, smooth-swinging lefty stepped into the batter's box and stared intently back at the pitcher. Our whole family sat together in the stands watching Logan with anticipation. Logan had always been an excellent baseball player, but tonight felt different; it felt like something special was about to happen.

The pitcher gripped the baseball tightly in his mitt, stepped through his windup, and hurled the ball toward home plate. In the blink of an eye, Logan located the ball and swung his bat with all his might. Then...*crack!* Logan hit the ball squarely, and, like a rocket, it took off high into the night sky. He ran toward first base watching the ball sail farther and farther, motioning as he ran for the ball to keep traveling. The outfielder raced toward the right field fence before watching hopelessly as the ball disappeared well beyond it—Logan's first ever home run!

Logan's smile was visible from the stands as he slowed into a victorious trot around the bases. Everyone in the crowd stood to celebrate the feat—everyone except our dad, Charley. While the rest of the crowd was cheering, Dad was running. He was running to hopefully find and retrieve this first home run ball to return to Logan. Dad bounded out of the bleachers and sped around the fence line toward right field. As he made the turn around the back of the bleachers, he spotted another young boy running in the same direction. The boy looked over his shoulder to see our dad barreling toward him, and he kicked it into high gear. The race was on! Dad burst into a full sprint giving everything he had to pass the boy and be the first to arrive at this home run ball. As the boy neared ever closer, our dad let out a desperate yell, "Don't get that ball! That's my son's first home run!" And to Dad's surprise, in an act of maturity beyond his years, the young boy stopped his running and allowed our now fairly winded but proud father to retrieve the ball. Logan's first home run ball could now be returned to its proper owner and displayed proudly in the Cain house for years to come.

The love of a father can make him do some wild things—like putting his children's needs before his own; like denying himself to ensure his children lack nothing; and like breaking into a full sprint to outpace a random kid and retrieve a first home run ball. Yet as valiant as an earthly father's love may appear, how much more is our heavenly Father's love for us?

Our God in heaven, knowing the pain and discomfort in store, lovingly sent Jesus into the world to live a sinless life we could not live, to die a death on the cross that we rightfully deserved, and to rise again and conquer death for all of us. There will never be a greater love than the love of God our Father.

Reflection Questions

- *What is the greatest gift or act of love you've ever received from a parent or parent figure? What did that mean to you?*
- *Scripture tells us that our love for one another cannot even compare to God's love toward us. When you think about the love your family has for one another, what feelings does that give you regarding God's love?*
- *How have you personally experienced the love of God?*

Activity

Sometimes, we can lose sight of all the amazing gifts God has given us. He gives countless good gifts to those who ask Him. As a family, start a "Gratefulness List" this week! On a piece of paper, write down everyone's name in a single column. Each day of the week, each member of the family is to write down a different gift from God for which they're grateful. At the end of the week, look back at this list and praise God as a family for all He's done!

People Helping People

Scripture
Galatians 6:1–2

¹ *Dear brothers and sisters, if another believer is overcome by*
some sin, you who are godly should gently and humbly help that
person back onto the right path. And be careful not to fall into
the same temptation yourself. ² *Share each other's burdens, and*
in this way obey the law of Christ.

The "Big Girl" Bed (Logan)

Taylor is the firstborn of us Cain children, which means she was
Mom and Dad's first attempt at this whole "parenting" thing. Taylor
brought so much life and love to the mix. She was a smart, talk-
ative child with a complete mind of her own and always kept our
folks on their toes. She was a near perfect child until ... bedtime .
For whatever reason, Taylor did not respond well to the concept of
sleeping alone in her big girl bed. So, night after night, she would
delay going to sleep, cry, and request to sleep in between our mom
and dad. And there are only so many sleepless nights a parent
can withstand fighting this battle before you just give in, tuck the
upset child in the center of your bed, and go back to sleep. So
Taylor, much to her delight, had become a permanent fixture in

our parents' bed each night. Then along came baby number two, Madison.

As Madison grew, Mom and Dad knew that Taylor's bedtime hijinks had to come to an end. There was no way they could squeeze another human into the same bed! But they also knew that Taylor wouldn't give up her position without some serious convincing. So they came up with an idea. They would task Taylor with "helping" young Madison sleep in her own big girl bed by sleeping in a big girl bed right next to her. Taylor had the chance to be the example for her younger sister to follow, and to show this new kid the ropes on how to handle bedtime. It would take bravery on Taylor's part to overcome her bedtime fears, but her desire to rise to the occasion was even stronger than her fear. With this new sense of responsibility and duty to our sister, Taylor thrived. For the first night ever, Taylor didn't fuss nor fight, but she took Madison to their bedroom, climbed into her own big girl bed, and made herself the example for Madison to follow.

Mom and Dad's plan worked! The girls were now both sleeping confidently in their beds and their own rest was restored. While this plan was intended for children, it has become applicable for everyday life in our walk with God. If you're struggling with a certain part of life, as opposed to trying harder or striving more fervently, could the key to overcoming your struggles be to help someone else facing the same problem? Maybe we make our greatest progress when we take our focus off ourselves and do all that we can to help others.

Reflection Questions

- *Have you ever noticed a person in your life struggling with something you used to wrestle with? What is a way that you could get involved to help?*
- *Scripture says to bear one another's burdens to fulfill the law of Christ (which boils down to loving the Lord with all your heart and loving your neighbor as yourself). What does it mean to you to bear someone's burdens?*
- *God's Word also warns not to fall into temptation yourself when you're helping someone walk through a challenging issue. What is a way you can protect yourself from falling into temptation?*

Activity

Today's activity is all about teamwork! Lay a blanket or bed sheet on the floor. Have every member of the family stand on the blanket/sheet. Without stepping off it or touching the floor, work together to flip over the blanket/sheet until everyone is standing on its other side. It'll take some skill to stay off the floor. Work together and see if you can do it!

Using Your Gifts

Scripture

1 Peter 4:10–11

[10] *God has given each of you a gift from his great variety of spiritual gifts. Use them well to serve one another.* [11] *Do you have the gift of speaking? Then speak as though God himself were speaking through you. Do you have the gift of helping others? Do it with all the strength and energy that God supplies. Then everything you do will bring glory to God through Jesus Christ. All glory and power to him forever and ever! Amen.*

Delivering a Miracle (Taylor)

In 2022, all of us Cain siblings and our spouses welcomed new babies into the world. First came baby River, daughter of Logan and his wife, Emily. Then in a few short months, it was baby Calloway, son of Madison and her husband, Jared, who was set to arrive. With this being their first child, both Madison and Jared spent the first day of labor in various states of worry and fear. Everything was new, everything felt foreign and scary, and if everything went well, they'd face the daunting responsibility of caring for a newborn baby. As much as they tried, they couldn't shake their fears about what lay ahead.

Emily was a practicing labor and delivery nurse at a local hospital, and she had helped women safely deliver children all the way up until she gave birth to River. On this day, she should have been resting. She should have been focused on her own infant, but when she learned of Madison and Jared's worries, she started putting together an overnight bag. She left her comforts of home and got to the hospital as quickly as she could. Then for the next day and a half, Emily ushered the presence of God into that hospital room. She used her nursing gifts and expertise to answer questions and bring a sense of calmness and understanding to my sister and brother-in-law. With every up and down throughout the delivery process, Emily was there to encourage and inform, and it changed the atmosphere of that room.

Madison ultimately had to be rushed to an emergency C-section when baby Calloway was unable to be delivered naturally. But thanks to Emily's guidance, Madison and Jared met this worrisome news with confidence. They trusted their medical team, followed through with the procedure, and within minutes, baby Calloway had safely entered the world. Emily packed up her things and went back home to her own new baby and husband with a feeling of great joy and accomplishment because she was able to help so greatly.

The next day, Emily met her new nephew and held him close with tears in her eyes. Madison and Jared had tears in their eyes too, because without Emily, baby Calloway's entry into the world would have been unbearably frightening. As the scriptures above teach us, Emily used the gifts God had given her to serve others, and not only did she bring great comfort to Madison and Jared, but she also brought glory to God through Jesus Christ.

Reflection Questions

- *What gifts do you feel the Lord has given to you? How could you use those gifts to positively influence someone else?*
- *How does using your gifts to help others glorify God?*

Activity

Time to put your family talents on display with a Talent Show! Take a moment for everyone to prepare a talent to share. You could perform a dance routine, display a unique skill, or anything in between! There's no talent too small or too big for this show. Have fun!

....

....

....

....

....

....

....

....

....

....

....

....

When the Music Fades

Scripture

Habakkuk 3:17–19

[17] Even though the fig trees have no blossoms, and there are no grapes on the vines; even though the olive crop fails, and the fields lie empty and barren; even though the flocks die in the fields, and the cattle barns are empty, [18] yet I will rejoice in the Lord! I will be joyful in the God of my salvation! [19] The Sovereign Lord is my strength!

Technical Difficulties (Taylor)

In 2023, CAIN the band set out on our first ever headlining music tour. We hit the road and were leading exhilarating nights of worship at churches all over the country. Being the headline band, however, meant that we were responsible for every detail of the tour. We had to find the right sound equipment, the right stage elements, and the right lights and video screens. We also had to assemble a team that could set up and operate all the equipment needed to put on a proper concert. There were so many details to account for, and so much pressure on us for everything to run smoothly.

Much to our relief, the tour started out perfectly! The shows were going great and people were enjoying these nights of worship.

That was until show number ten. For whatever reason, everything that could go wrong that night went wrong. During the opening song, all the video screens completely turned off. This was a startling change for the audience reading the lyrics on the screens so they could sing along with the music. But nothing was more startling than when the full sound system completely turned off. All the music disappeared: no guitars, no piano, no microphones for singers. The auditorium fell awkwardly silent.

Both we and our production team scrambled to figure out what had gone wrong. We feverishly unplugged cables and flipped circuit breakers, but no matter what measures we took, we couldn't get the sound equipment to turn back on. It appeared that the show was about to become a total loss, so our team huddled backstage while the audience began to stir uncomfortably. The team threw out their opinions on the situation. Some thought we just needed to cancel the concert, and some wanted to continue trying to repair the problem. While the team was deliberating, Logan walked out on stage with an acoustic guitar. The crowd fell quiet as they looked to him for direction. With a loud voice—since he didn't have a working microphone—Logan delivered the news to the audience. "Everyone, we're so sorry, but we seem to be experiencing some technical difficulties. Thank you for your patience." But then, before he could share any additional bad news, Logan felt the Lord leading him in a different direction.

"It seems like nothing is going to go right this evening," Logan shouted. "But I know one thing: whether the show runs smoothly or not, whether the sound equipment works or not, our God is good and worthy of our praise. We don't have to have any speakers or microphones to worship Him together tonight." Logan strummed on his guitar and lifted a song of praise to God. Before he knew it, the entire audience joined in and raised their voices in singing. The sanctuary boomed with the sound of over a thousand voices joined together worshipping God.

At the end of this impromptu song, the audience erupted in applause for their heavenly Father, and lo and behold, the sound equipment began working properly again! The show continued as planned, but the most powerful moment of the night was when the music faded away, all seemed lost, and instead of being upset, everyone chose to praise God in a tough situation.

Reflection Questions

- *Do you remember a time when it seemed like everything that could go wrong, went wrong? How did you respond in that moment?*
- *What does it look like practically to be joyful in a challenging situation? What things can you think about to help you keep that mindset?*

Activity

Now you get to experience some audio technical difficulties of your own. It's time for a family game of charades. Without speaking, one family member is to try to act out a movie, book, or object of their choice. Based on their movements, the other family members try to guess what is being acted out. Everyone take turns being both the actor and a guesser.

DAY 12

Secret Preparation

Scripture

David and Goliath • 1 Samuel 17:34–37 ESV

[34] *But David said to Saul, "Your servant used to keep sheep for his father. And when there came a lion, or a bear, and took a lamb from the flock,* [35] *I went after him and struck him and delivered it out of his mouth. And if he arose against me, I caught him by his beard and struck him and killed him.* [36] *Your servant has struck down both lions and bears, and this uncircumcised Philistine [Goliath] shall be like one of them, for he has defied the armies of the living God."* [37] *And David said, "The Lord who delivered me from the paw of the lion and from the paw of the bear will deliver me from the hand of this Philistine."*

Shari's Secret Skill (Logan)

One thing our family really enjoys is some friendly competition. From shooting basketball to throwing frisbee, anything and everything can be turned into a way to compete with one another. One such competition took a rather surprising turn. While enjoying some time together outside, the men of the Cain family started to casually shoot a BB gun at a safely positioned target. We boys were trying to aim our shots carefully to hit the inner rings of the target. Quickly, the casual shooting became an accuracy contest. Each shooter went back and forth trying to outperform the others.

As the contest intensified, our mom, Shari, strolled up to the group. She watched quietly for a few rounds before one of us asked if she'd like to try her hand at the competition. Shari accepted the offer, although she admitted she didn't have much experience with a BB gun. She raised the gun toward the target, peered down the sites, and pulled the trigger . . . bullseye. She hit the center of the target, a feat that none of us had managed. She readied a second BB, took aim and fired again . . . another bullseye. By this point, our jaws were nearly touching the ground. How was she this good of a shot? After her *third* bullseye, it was apparent that the competition was over by a landslide. Mom was far and away the most accurate shooter of the bunch.

"I thought you said you didn't have much experience shooting a BB gun," one of the guys asked. Shari replied, "That's right! I don't have much experience shooting *BB* guns, but I do have lots of experience shooting. I was on the competitive shooting team in high school."

Again, we were stunned. All along Mom possessed this secret skill that blew us all away. Unbeknownst to her, in her years of training and practicing, she was preparing to absolutely crush her son and sons-in-law in a friendly family competition someday.

Similarly in Scripture, for years David faithfully tended to his father's sheep. While he was there, alone in the fields, God was preparing him for his future. He wrote songs and prayed to the Lord, and he honed his skills with his sling to protect the sheep against wild animals. When the moment was right, David used all his "secret skills" to conquer mighty Goliath and set the table for him to one day become the king of Israel. Like David, may we be faithful to remain prepared in private for what God plans to do through us in public.

Reflection Questions

- *Unbeknownst to David, when he was tending sheep in his father's field, God was secretly preparing him for great things ahead. Have you ever felt like you were just "tending sheep in a field"? What do you feel like God was teaching you in that time?*
- *Life will undoubtedly bring its challenges to us. What are some practical ways you can stay prepared to follow the Lord through it all?*

Activity

It's your turn for a little friendly, family competition. Crumple up enough sheets of paper for each person to have five paper wads. Set a small bucket or waste basket in one corner of the room. Each family member will attempt to throw their paper wads across the room and into the basket. The person who makes the most shots wins! Change things up in a fun way by trying to distract the other players while they're throwing. Make funny sounds, wave your arms wildly, whatever it takes to throw them off their game! May the best player win!

Practicing Perseverance

Scripture

James 1:2–4 NIV

> 2 *Consider it pure joy, my brothers and sisters, whenever you face trials of many kinds,* 3 *because you know that the testing of your faith produces perseverance.* 4 *Let perseverance finish its work so that you may be mature and complete, not lacking anything.*

Logan & Emily's Golden Moment (Taylor)

Logan and his wife, Emily, aren't your average parents of small children. They have a hidden talent that only a fraction of people possess, and that talent is cheerleading. You would have no clue just by looking at them that Logan can hurl Emily high into the air while Emily flips gracefully and lands with one foot into Logan's upraised hand. While that sounds terrifying to most people, to Logan and Emily it's fun ... and it's a way of life.

Logan and Emily met and eventually fell in love thanks to the world of cheerleading. Logan was a new cheerleader, learning the basics of gymnastics and cheer stunting at our south Alabama college, Troy University. As Logan learned the sport, he quickly became enamored and wanted to train with the world's best cheerleaders to sharpen his skills. That's when he met the best cheerleader in the world ... Emily.

Emily was a collegiate national champion at the elite University of Kentucky and a gold-medal-winning cheerleader for the Team USA cheerleading team. If there was an accolade to win in the world of cheer, she'd won it . . . twice. Logan was introduced to Emily prior to the tryouts for Team USA, and he quickly realized that to be the best, he needed to work with her. Emily agreed to train with Logan and help him earn a position on the team, and what unfolded was many months of tireless work.

The duo worked together nearly every day. They traveled hours to meet one another to practice their cheerleading stunts, they exercised hard to stay in great shape, and they persevered through injuries and setbacks along the way. They knew that all their work would boil down to one brief tryout. They'd have one chance to impress the coaches and earn the opportunity to cheer for Team USA. That tall task brought great stress on them both, but they turned that stress into determination. When they felt nervous about their tryout, instead of sitting in fear, they would get together and practice. They really began to enjoy the work! They considered this physically and mentally trying time to be a season of joy.

Then finally, Logan and Emily arrived at the big day of Team USA tryouts with excitement and anticipation. They had worked and prepared themselves as much as humanly possible and persevered through all the grueling days of training. When the time came for their tryout, they executed their stunts flawlessly ... and both made the USA cheerleading team!

But above all else, they had developed a tenacity that no trial could ever diminish. That same tenacity would see them all the way to winning back-to-back gold medals at the World Cheer Competition. And eventually their grit would help them tackle any relational trial they could ever face as they fell in love and married one another in 2019. All along the way, the Lord was instilling in them a perseverance and strength that reached beyond cheerleading and helped make them more like their Savior, Jesus.

Reflection Questions

- *Have you ever had to demonstrate perseverance in your life? What were the circumstances? What was the result of your effort?*
- *The scripture from James says that the testing of our faith produces this perseverance. Have you ever felt like your faith was being tested? What happened, and how did you respond? How did you see God differently at the end of that time?*

Activity

Time to take some family inventory. Get a piece of paper and mark a straight line down the center. On the left side of the line, write a trial that was a challenge for your family. On the right side of the line, write how God came through to help you endure that time. Some of your family's challenges may still be ongoing. After you finish your list, pray together, thanking God for how He's helped you in the past and seeking perseverance for any ongoing challenges.

Listen to Wisdom

Scripture

James 1:22–25 NIV

22 Do not merely listen to the word, and so deceive yourselves. Do what it says. 23 Anyone who listens to the word but does not do what it says is like someone who looks at his face in a mirror 24 and, after looking at himself, goes away and immediately forgets what he looks like. 25 But whoever looks intently into the perfect law that gives freedom, and continues in it—not forgetting what they have heard, but doing it—they will be blessed in what they do.

The Bird House (Madison)

After my husband, Jared, and I were married we saved every penny we could for a few years, and then, thankfully, we were able to purchase our first home together. It was a modest, 1960s-era ranch-style house with lots of "character," which we now know is just a fancy word for "issues." We were eager to make this little house our home, so we got started right away on several pressing projects. We knocked down walls, changed out flooring, and painted every square inch of the house. Then we worked on the crown jewel of the home, the large stone fireplace. This fireplace was stunning, but to our surprise, the previous owner had sealed a heavy tile over the top of the chimney and hadn't used the fireplace in years.

Jared asked our new next-door neighbor if he knew why this tile was put in place, and the neighbor had an interesting answer. "The owner put that tile up because birds kept flying down the chimney and getting into the house." Jared was taken aback; he certainly wasn't expecting that bizarre answer. "Well, we want to use the fireplace, so I think we'll be taking the tile down," Jared replied confidently. The neighbor retorted, "Okay, but you better do something to keep the birds from getting in or you'll be in the same boat as the last folks."

Jared climbed to the top of the chimney, removed the heavy tile from the opening, and proceeded to open the fireplace for business. In the back of my mind I thought, *Although it's not likely, we better install a guard on this chimney, so no birds get inside.* But our neighbor's wise recommendation fell lower and lower on the priority list, and eventually we forgot about it entirely. That was until one wild night.

Returning home from a date on the town, we couldn't wait to get back to our cozy fireplace and unwind with a funny TV show. When we entered the house, something seemed "off." Otter, our typically lazy French bulldog, was standing awkwardly in the center of the living room. His eyes were wide and he appeared to be frozen in place. He didn't greet us at the door like he normally did. When we got closer we realized his wide-eyed gaze was fixed on the living room wall. That's when we saw *it*.

There, clinging to the wall, was a small black object. We inched closer and closer until we could make out feathers and a small beak. "Wait a minute, is that a bir..." was all that Jared could utter before this unwanted house guest spread its wings and began to fly wildly around the room. Jared, Otter, and I ran screaming in three different directions. "There's a bird in the house!" I shouted. Jared, who hadn't realized he had a fear of birds until this moment, ran to an entirely different room while the little black bird flew around the kitchen dropping "presents" with every flap of its wings.

We watched around a corner as the bird settled into its new resting place near the back door. After mustering all our courage, we ran to the back door and flung it wide open. To our surprise, the bird flew right out and away from the house. As quickly as the terrifying intruder had appeared, he was gone!

While we can look back on this moment and laugh today, we learned an ever-valuable lesson: if you get wise advice—like *put a guard on your chimney so a scary bird doesn't fly into your house*—don't just listen to it, act on it! James in his epistle relates this same sentiment when talking about the Word of God. He challenges us not just to hear the perfect wisdom of God's Word but to let it guide our behavior...and we will be blessed in all that we do.

Reflection Questions

- *Has anyone ever given you great advice, maybe when you were younger? What was it, and did you act on that advice? If not, do you wish you had?*

- *Today's scripture says to not be merely* hearers *of God's Word but* doers. *What makes it difficult to "do" God's Word in our everyday lives? How can you be a better doer of God's Word at work or school this week?*

Activity

Now you can try your hand at being a bird with the Baby Bird Race! All you need are two bowls and a bag of small food items (marshmallows, pretzels, small candies, etc. will do!). Place one bowl across the room and dump all of the chosen food into it. Place the other bowl on the opposite side of the room and leave it empty. Each family member will take turns running to the bowl of food and picking up a single piece of food with their mouth. Then the family member will race back and use their mouth to drop the food into the empty bowl. See how many pieces of food each family member can get into the bowl in one minute! The family member who puts the most food into the bowl wins!

....

....

....

....

....

....

....

....

....

....

....

Waste Not, Want Not

Scripture

Proverbs 13:4

⁴ *Lazy people want much but get little, but those who work hard will prosper.*

Proverbs 21:5 NIV

⁵ *The plans of the diligent lead to profit as surely as haste leads to poverty.*

Luke 16:10

¹⁰ *"If you are faithful in little things, you will be faithful in large ones."*

A Perfectly Good Tape (Madison)

From our earliest memories, we Cains have always had a love for Christmas music, and we had the most love for the Christmas music of Amy Grant. When we were all young, our father, Charley, purchased an Amy Grant Christmas cassette tape for our family to enjoy. (Kids, have your parents explain what a "cassette tape" is.) We listened to this tape over and over and over again. It was the soundtrack of our holiday season . . . until one day, the music stopped.

Dad popped the cassette tape out of the stereo for a proper examination. After years of heavy use, the small roll of tape inside the cassette that held our musical favorites had broken apart. To an ordinary person, this damage would spell the end of this cassette. An ordinary person would toss that tape in the trash and head to the store to purchase another. But Charley Cain is no ordinary person. What most would consider a lost cause, he considered a worthy challenge.

Dad took the cassette to the garage and over to his work-bench. He carefully unwound the tape and removed it from the cassette. He saw the tear in the tape, plain as day. If only he could put the tape back together it had a chance of working again. With surgical precision, Dad carefully glued the torn ends of the tape back together. After allowing the glue to dry, he rewound the tape into the cassette, and then came the moment of truth. He popped the cassette back into the stereo, pressed play, and reveled in the sweet holiday melodies of Amy Grant once again! Dad had fixed the cassette, and we were delighted to be able to keep singing along to our favorite songs.

If Dad had gone to the store to buy a new cassette tape, that wouldn't have been the wrong thing to do. But he wanted to take this opportunity to demonstrate for us that something worth having is worth working for. If you have the means and the deter-mination to fix something on your own—go for it! Hard work is never wasted, and it's important to be faithful over even the smallest of things God has given you.

The cassette tape brought enjoyment to our family for several more years after that day. And for the rest of its life, there was a subtle skip in the music when the repaired section of the cassette tape was amplified over the stereo speakers. This little skip would become a cherished memory for us all, a reminder of our dad's hard work and the strong example he set for us.

Reflection Questions

- *Jesus shares a parable in Luke 16 about a shrewd manager. That's where He challenges that if you are faithful in little things, you'll be faithful in large things as well. What does that mean to you? What is an example of how you can be faithful in the little things God has given you?*
- *Are there some places in your life where laziness has set in? Share with your family and commit to helping one another overcome laziness and be good stewards of your blessings, your time, etc.*

Activity

The Skipping Cassette: This is a music-based game! Grab a phone, CD, or other device that can play music. One family member will start playing one of their favorite songs for the rest of the family on that device. Then, at a random moment in the song, the first person will stop the music and challenge the other family members to continue singing the next line from memory. Whoever can recite the next line of the song properly, wins! The winner gets to pick the next song for everyone to try! Play a few rounds and see if your family can guess the lyrics!

Be Transformed

Scripture

Romans 12:2

² *Don't copy the behavior and customs of this world, but let God transform you into a new person by changing the way you think. Then you will learn to know God's will for you, which is good and pleasing and perfect.*

The Impact of One Bulb (Taylor)

While Christmastime at the Cain house means several fun holiday traditions, one of our holiday traditions is *not* so fun. That would be the annual Christmas Light Bulb Checking Party. This event is marked by what feels like hundreds of plastic grocery bags scattered all over the house, each containing a string of Christmas lights that may be one year old or twenty years old—nothing is ever thrown away. Every family member grabs bags of lights and parks themself beside an available wall power outlet, and one by one, we plug the strings into the wall to determine if they're still working. What if the lights don't turn on when you plug them in? Do you bag them up and throw them away? Of course not! You grab a tiny, spare Christmas light bulb and plug it into *every* light socket on that string until, hopefully, the whole string of lights illuminates again.

This is a rather tedious process, but more often than not, a single blown bulb can make the entire string of lights seem like it too is blown. It is wild what a large impact one little bulb can make. While this task is monotonous, taking the time to search each string of lights for defective bulbs has allowed the Cain family Christmas lights to far outlive the lights of many holiday decorators. But in the monotony, in the painstaking replacement of small light bulbs, there is an important lesson.

We, too, have a bright light inside of us. We have the Savior of the world, Jesus Christ, living in our hearts. We have the Holy Spirit guiding our steps and helping us bring the hope of Jesus to a desperate world. In today's verse from Romans, Paul instructed not to be conformed to the behavior and customs of the world. The world and its desires are often far from God. The things that the world places value in aren't valuable to Him. The things the world deems acceptable and good often contradict what God has spelled out in His Word. The world, in essence, can be like a burned-out light bulb on a string of Christmas lights. And if we look to the world for our cues on how to act, how to speak, and how to treat others, we will find ourselves looking just like the world: burned out with no light in us.

So we must not be conformed to match the world, but we must let God transform us into a new person by changing the way we think! We must look to the example of Jesus—how He inter-acted with others, what He deemed important—and emulate that behavior. Then the light that shines in us will be bright for all to see. And those around us who are hurting or lost will come to *us* to ask how they can find that light.

Reflection Questions

- *What is one way that God has transformed the way you think? Did you have a perspective prior to your relationship with Jesus that has changed since coming to know Him?*
- *What is one way you've felt the world trying to conform you to its standards of right and wrong?*
- *What can you do as a family to help one another not copy the world and instead allow God to make you more like Jesus?*

Activity

There is a powerful object lesson used in modern-day churches called a cardboard testimony. Today, you can try this out as a family! All you need is either an 8" x 10" piece of cardboard or a blank sheet of paper for each family member. Everyone will take a marker or pen and on one side of the cardboard/paper write or draw the way that they used to be before they met Jesus. Then, on the opposite side of the cardboard/paper, each will write or draw how they show God's heart more now because of Jesus. Maybe you used to tell lies, but since meeting Jesus you tell the truth. Or maybe you used to live in fear, but Jesus has made you courageous. Make your cardboard testimony and share it with your family.

God's Handiwork

Scripture

Romans 1:20

[20] *For ever since the world was created, people have seen the earth and sky. Through everything God made, they can clearly see his invisible qualities—his eternal power and divine nature. So they have no excuse for not knowing God.*

Psalm 95:4-5

[4] *He holds in his hands the depths of the earth and the mightiest mountains.* [5] *The sea belongs to him, for he made it. His hands formed the dry land, too.*

Cal's First Beach Day (Madison)

The beach has always been a sacred place to me. The warm sun, the white sand, the rhythmic crashing waves—all these things bring me so much joy and peace. When my husband, Jared, and I had our first child, our son Calloway, I secretly hoped that our new baby boy would one day love the beach as much as I did. Just before Cal's first birthday, the opportunity arose to put this secret desire to the test. Our whole family decided to take a vacation to the beach and let our new little ones experience the coast for the first time.

Based on appearances alone, you would assume Calloway has hardly seen the sun, much less spent time on the beach. Cal has very fair, sensitive skin paired with light red hair—all the makings for sunburn, windburn, and a miserable beach experience. I made every accommodation to help ensure Cal had a great time. Heavy-duty baby sunscreen, a long sleeve swim shirt, a large sun hat, dark sunglasses, a baby-sized shade tent . . . you name it, I brought it to help make Cal's first experience as smooth as can be. I was ready for anything . . . except for what actually happened.

As Jared and I carried Cal and his wealth of beach supplies toward the boardwalk, the smell of the salty sea air greeted us. We climbed the boardwalk steps higher and higher until we stood at the top, with a picturesque expanse of white sand and crystal-clear blue water rolling in to the shore. I looked to see Cal's face, and his smile was already glowing from ear to ear. This was only the beginning for little Cal; he loved everything about the beach. He loved swimming in the water, he loved playing in the sand, and he loved the warmth of the sun. He wanted to go back and forth between splashing in the ocean with Jared and scooping up handfuls of sand on the beach. Cal even went as far as to lie down face-first in the warm sand over and over. Every time we turned around he was either covered in sand from head to toe or drenched in salt water, all the while smiling and laughing. There is loving the beach and then there is *Calloway* loving the beach.

Cal's love for his first day on the beach reinvigorated all our love for the beach. His eyes kept lighting up as he took in all of God's creation. Everything was amazing, everything was beautiful, and everything was worthy of recognition. It made us all slow down and look around

The God of the universe, in His infinite power and wisdom, made these gorgeous beaches with just a word. He spoke them into being, and their beauty and peacefulness reflect His goodness. The constant, rolling waves reflect His faithfulness; He's always there for us in every moment. He was mighty and capable enough to create this part of nature, but He's also tender and thoughtful enough to know the hairs on our heads and every detail of our lives. Sometimes it takes the eyes and excitement of a child to remind us of the glory of God shining all around us.

Reflection Questions

- *What part of God's creation is your favorite? The beach, the mountains, the desert, something else? How is God's glory shown through your favorite part of creation?*
- *What practical steps can you take as a family to slow down and recognize God's handiwork all around you?*

Activity

Weather permitting, head outside as a family. Take a moment and look at the things all around you. Give everyone a turn to share what parts of God's creation stick out to them. Pray as a family and praise God for the mighty work of His hands.

....

....

....

....

Run the Race

Scripture

Hebrews 12:1–2

[1] *Therefore, since we are surrounded by such a huge crowd of witnesses to the life of faith, let us strip off every weight that slows us down, especially the sin that so easily trips us up. And let us run with endurance the race God has set before us.* [2] *We do this by keeping our eyes on Jesus, the champion who initiates and perfects our faith.*

Cain Family Field Day (Logan)

Our family was a proud homeschooling family, but early on, when Taylor was five and Madison and I weren't quite old enough for school, Taylor attended a public elementary school for kindergarten. While it was a short-lived experience and certainly not her favorite place in the world, Taylor still managed to experience the wonderment that was a public-school Field Day. Three-legged races, potato-sack races, egg tosses, blue ribbons: it was all so much fun for Taylor. She came home to Madison and me and told us all about the fun time she'd had.

With every amazing detail she revealed, we felt more and more left out. We both wished we had gotten to experience Field Day as well. To our surprise, our parents, Charley and Shari, were listening in on Taylor's rundown. Mom and Dad made eye contact and had the same idea in mind: *Why don't we make our own Field Day?* They sprung to action and gathered up some essential supplies: two broomsticks, three garbage bags, three eggs, and three spoons. Before you knew it, the Cain Family Field Day was up and running.

Mom and Dad called us kids outside to reveal what they had created, and we were thrilled! One by one, we completed the various events. There was the long jump competition, which had us leaping across two broomsticks laid across the grass. There was the garbage bag "potato sack" race. And there was the ever-challenging egg-in-spoon relay race. We all had an absolute ball at our very own Field Day, and no longer did little Madison and I feel left out of the fun.

Hearing of Taylor running a race at school made her siblings long to run a race of our own, and isn't that a beautiful metaphor for our walk with Jesus? Like Madison and me watching and emulating Taylor, we all are surrounded by a great cloud of witnesses as we walk out our faith in Jesus. When we lay aside the sins and bad habits that hold us back, we can lead our lives with such honor and integrity that other people will be inspired to run their own races well. And along the way, as we keep our focus fixed on Jesus, the Lord matures and perfects our faith.

Reflection Questions

- *The writer of Hebrews describes the life of a Jesus follower as a "race" that God has set before us. In this scripture, what does the writer say we must do in order to run this race well?*

- *How does keeping your eyes on Jesus help increase your faith and your strength to endure?*
- *Do you feel like there is a weight (a struggle, a bad habit, a fear, etc.) slowing you down in the race of life? Pray with your family to ask for help in stripping off this weight so you can run the race with endurance.*

Activity

You're never too old for your own family Field Day! Get outside and let the games begin! Here are some Field Day game ideas your family can try:

- *Foot Race*
- *Jump the Brook: Lay two broomsticks on the ground a slight distance apart and have every family member try to jump over the gap between the two sticks. Each round scoot the broomsticks farther from each other. If someone's foot touches the ground between the broomsticks, they're out!*
- *Three-Legged-Race: Grab a partner and tie your ankles together using a cloth bandana. Work together to carefully run a race while your legs are in tandem.*
- *Egg Toss: Grab a partner and a raw egg. Carefully toss the egg to one another without breaking its shell. With each throw, scoot farther away from one another to increase the difficulty in safely catching the egg. Last team to break their egg wins!*

Nurturing a Calling

Scripture

1 Timothy 4:12

[12] *Don't let anyone think less of you because you are young. Be an example to all believers in what you say, in the way you live, in your love, your faith, and your purity.*

Sunday Morning Talent Show (Madison)

"Dad, I think I'm ready to give a word to the church," said I, a nine-year-old who was not qualified in any way to "give a word" to the church. This was our childhood. As the pastor's kids, we were handed a specific type of nepotism—we were given the church. The church instruments were ours to practice on, the youth room hosted our birthday parties, and the church parking lot was for learning to drive. But most useful of all, we got to test out our latest inspirations on the church congregation.

Taylor, Logan, and I would get a random inspiration and immediately ask our dad, "Can we sing a special song on Sunday morning?" or, "We just made up a special dance. Can we do it for church?" He let us every time we asked. I imagine the church members must have rolled their eyes when, Sunday after Sunday, they had to sit through the Cain children talent show before they could hear a good sermon. But looking back, my parents' open-handedness with their calling was the very thing that prepared us for the calling we have now. As part of our band CAIN, we are constantly on a stage, "giving a word" and making up a song and dance. God put this desire in our hearts, and our parents helped us nurture that gift.

Now I'm a mom to a beautiful one-year-old boy. I'm in the throes of feeding him, teaching him his ABCs, and keeping him alive. But today's verse reminds me that God has big plans for Calloway. I will give him access to everything I have to help him walk in that, just like my parents did for me. Parents, look at your children. Who they'll become one day, the future God has for them, is already inside of them right now! You have the precious opportunity to use what you have to nurture that gifting.

Reflection Questions

- *What are some traits/characteristics you recognize in your children that are uniquely them? Do you see a glimpse into their future?*
- *Kids, what are some ways you can use your talents now instead of waiting until you're older?*

Activity

"Preparing a Word": Everyone play the role of a Cain kid and take five to ten minutes to prepare something to share with your family. It can be a poem, a dance, a word of encouragement, a drawing, or even a joke. Get creative and take turns sharing your "word" with everyone.

Better For It

Scripture

Romans 5:3–5 NIV

³ *Not only so, but we also glory in our sufferings, because we know that suffering produces perseverance;* ⁴ *perseverance, character; and character, hope.* ⁵ *And hope does not put us to shame, because God's love has been poured out into our hearts through the Holy Spirit, who has been given to us.*

Mother's Day Out (Madison)

Tears were streaming down my face. I felt short of breath and full of panic. My son, Calloway, reached for me as we were pulled in different directions. What I'm describing was not any real emergency at all, but remembering it still brings a tear to my eye.

I had dropped Cal off at Mother's Day Out daycare. Other parents stared in confusion as I walked back to my car, my cries turning into a form of hiccups at this point. Before becoming a mom, I would have rolled my eyes at the idea that you can't spend a few hours away from your baby. I mean, get a grip! But even an hour after I dropped him off, I was still crying hot tears. I kept thinking, *He's so small. His backpack is the same size as his whole body. He doesn't know anyone. I am his home, and he doesn't understand that I'm coming back for him.* I was flooded with guilt that I was abandoning Calloway.

Months prior, my husband and I debated endlessly about whether we should put Cal in a Mother's Day Out program. We'd heard many stories of how programs like these help kids with language development and confidence, and frankly, we needed the childcare help. We made the choice to enroll him, not because it felt good but because we knew it was *for* his good. We wanted to help our son grow!

This situation gave new meaning to Romans 5:3–5, the passage quoted above. We can have confidence walking through things that *feel* bad when they truly *are* good, because the Holy Spirit is building character in us.

We picked up Cal as soon as daycare let out on his first day, and to our surprise, he got sent home with a great report card. He overcame his tears and settled in nicely, playing with the other children in his class. He even managed to take a sturdy, two-hour nap during their allotted nap time. We were proud of our boy ... and we were proud of ourselves too. We all had made it through our first taste of daycare, and we were stronger than ever before.

Reflection Questions

- *Talk about things that feel "bad" but are "good," like exercising, eating vegetables, or taking medicine. What are the benefits of doing these things—especially since often our first instinct is to avoid them?*
- *When was a time that you were nervous to try something new? What happened? Were you better off because of the experience?*

Activity

What is a new family tradition you can start that may feel "bad" at first but is truly "good" for you? Maybe it's a family jog on Saturday mornings, or a day of the week spent with no phones or TV. No matter what it is, there is always a new tradition you can start that will be for your ultimate good. Think about what this could be as a family, and get started today!

....

....

....

....

....

....

....

....

....

....

....

....

....

....

....

Young Love

Scripture
Psalm 37:4; 23–24

⁴ *Take delight in the Lord, and he will give you your heart's desires.*
²³ *The Lord directs the steps of the godly. He delights in every detail of their lives.* ²⁴ *Though they stumble, they will never fall, for the Lord holds them by the hand.*

Charley + Shari 4-Ever (Taylor)

What do Christian people even do *on weekends?* Charley thought as he drove north from his college town in Alabama. This was the beginning of a new chapter. He had spent most of his young adult life avoiding all things church, but after experiencing all the world had to offer, he was empty inside. It was in his last week of college that he gave his life to the Lord with a simple but life-changing sentence: "God, if you'll have me, I'll spend the rest of my life telling people about you."

In that instant, a new Charley was born. His desires changed, and he had one goal: to follow the Lord wherever He might lead and tell as many folks as he could about Jesus. He was driving north to Tennessee for one his first few "Christian" activities. He'd always played guitar and sang, but this weekend he was set to lead worship for a young adult gathering. His only expectation was to play songs about Jesus, but the Lord had even more in store.

Shari was fixing her hair and contemplating whether she was actually going to this young adult gathering. Her friends from church were all going, and apparently some college guy from Alabama was coming to lead worship, but she was still uncertain. Shari wasn't exactly raised in a Christian home, but after experiencing a Fellowship of Christian Athletes summer camp in high school, she fell in love with the message of the gospel and gave her life to Jesus. After that she started getting rides with friends to church and learning all that she could about the Lord.

After waffling a bit, she decided to just get dressed and go see what this young adult gathering was all about. At the very least she could see some friends and hear some music. When she walked into the local coffeehouse where the event was held, the worship music was about to begin. So she pressed ahead all the way to the front row. That's when her eyes met those of the mysterious college guy leading worship ... Charley.

Little did they know the impact that first look would have on the rest of their lives and on countless others. They likely couldn't tell you any of the songs that were played that night because they were so surprised at the instant connection they felt. As soon as the music stopped, Charley made his way to Shari and proceeded to pour on the perfect amount of charm. He learned that Shari had been homecoming queen, so he used a pretzel stick as a microphone and interviewed her as if she had just won the Miss America pageant. They laughed, they smiled, and they got lost in great conversation. Before they were ready to leave, the gathering was starting to disperse, so they quickly exchanged addresses and home telephone numbers (kids, ask your parents about this part). What unfolded was a precious season of the two lovebirds exchanging heartfelt letters and frequent phone calls, and then Charley making more and more drives up to Tennessee.

Their love grew stronger until it was evident that God meant for them to be together forever. Charley and Shari were married in 1985, and so began the building of a beautiful life. There was no coincidence in this story. They met one another by following God and allowing Him to guide their steps, and He continually gave them the desires of their heart, as today's scriptures say. Year after year, they'd listen for His voice and step faithfully into what God laid before them.

God proceeded to lay before them a beautiful marriage, kingdom-building opportunities, and a mutual heart for hurting people in need of shepherds. Eventually He laid before them the chance to raise children of their own. Each time they stepped out in faith, and each time their decisions changed the eternities of countless people. Thank God for Charley and Shari Cain.

Reflection Questions

- *Compare your heart's desires before and after you met Jesus. Did the desires change? Did you desire something different for your life after you began your relationship with Jesus?*
- *God's Word says He holds us by the hand so that though we may stumble in life from time to time, we won't fall. What response does that elicit in you? How would that impact your decision-making if you knew God was holding you by the hand?*

Activity

Let's play a game that demonstrates the impact of God's hand in our lives. Everyone will need a paper plate and a marker. Each person places the plate on top of their head. During this game, everyone must keep their plate on top of their head and cannot take it down until the game is complete. Have someone read out the following commands:

- *Draw a house.*
- *Draw sunshine in the sky.*
- *Add a front door and windows to the house.*
- *Draw the front lawn.*
- *Add flowers to the lawn.*
- *Draw a smiling face on the sunshine.*
- *Add a tree to the front lawn.*
- *Draw yourself under the tree.*

Now, let everyone behold their artwork! The scenes will likely look pretty messy.

Next, play the game again, but this time choose partners. One person gets to be the artist, and the other gets to represent God's hands. Call out the drawing commands again, but this time the person acting as God's hands can help guide the artist's marker into a good position. Once complete, compare your first drawing to your second drawing, which was completed with the help of "God's hands." Did it help having someone to assist you who could see the whole picture? Just like in life, if we try to live on our own, without the Lord, we can make quite the mess. But if we trust in the Lord, He is faithful to guide us and help us along the way.

Help in Our Weakness

Scripture

Romans 8:26–28

[26] *And the Holy Spirit helps us in our weakness. For example, we don't know what God wants us to pray for. But the Holy Spirit prays for us with groanings that cannot be expressed in words.* [27] *And the Father who knows all hearts knows what the Spirit is saying, for the Spirit pleads for us believers in harmony with God's own will.* [28] *And we know that God causes everything to work together for the good of those who love God and are called according to His purpose for them.*

Who Needs a Fork? (Madison)

Have you ever spread yourself a little too thin? In the spring of 2023, our band had done just that. We had agreed to multiple great opportunities that just so happened to all fall on the exact same night. We were blessed with the opportunity to host Christian music's biggest night: the K-LOVE Fan Awards at the Grand Ole Opry. Hosting the awards was a dream opportunity that none of us could have ever fathomed. And it came with months of preparations. There were songs to write, dances to choreograph, outfits to organize, and more. We put our entire hearts into this chance to host, and we excitedly awaited the day of the awards! But hosting the awards wasn't the only item on our agenda that evening.

We had also previously accepted the opportunity to perform at the K-LOVE Fan Awards after-party aboard the General Jackson Showboat. This was going to be a late-night event, and we would be delivering two musical performances aboard this vessel for an expectant audience. We were honored to accept, but as the weight of hosting the awards show really set in, we three became increasingly worried that we'd overextended ourselves. Be that as it may, we resolved to honor our commitments and trust that the Holy Spirit would help us in our inevitable physical exhaustion.

Finally, the night of the Fan Awards arrived, and we prayed together before stepping out of our dressing room. "Father, above all else, tonight, with everything we say, we sing, we do, how we treat one another—we want to bring glory and honor to your name." Logan prayed with his arms wrapped around our shoulders. And when we walked onto that stage, we tried to do just that. All the preparation, all the prayer and thought that went into the awards show shined though, and it was a powerful night gathered with thousands of other believers. When we took our final bow, we immediately sprinted off stage, grabbed our after-party show outfits, and were whisked away to the nearby General Jackson.

Fatigue had fully set in—vocally, physically, and emotionally. Still, the three of us encouraged one another as we prepared for our final two performances of the night. "God has given us the strength to get this far, and He's not going to leave us now," Taylor spoke in faith before slipping her guitar over her shoulder. "We may be tired, but He is worthy of our praise. He's worthy of every last bit of energy we have." And that's exactly what we gave as an offering to the Lord. Every bit of our energy was poured into a passionate night of worship aboard the showboat. And as we hit our final notes, a wave of relief washed over each of us.

We made our way backstage to find a lovely barbecue dinner waiting in our dressing room—an amazing reward for a job well done. When we realized there was no silverware to be found, we didn't even panic; we simply sat cross-legged on the floor and ate barbecue with our hands. We smiled, and laughed, and ate, as thankful as can be. Although it may have been one of our messier dinners, it was the best meal we'd ever tasted. It would forever serve as a reminder of Paul's teaching in Romans that the Holy Spirit will always help us in our weakness. When we are weak, He is always, always strong.

Reflection Questions

- *Have you ever had a day where you felt stretched far too thin? What happened? How did that day work out?*
- *When you feel at your weakest, do you find it natural to call out to God for help? Or do you just try to push through on your own?*
- *What are some areas of weakness in your life that you recognize you need God's help to see you through?*

Activity

The Marshmallow Tower Challenge: For today's activity, you will use something weak to try and create something strong! All you'll need is a box of uncooked spaghetti noodles, a two-foot strip of tape (masking tape works best!), and a bag of roasting marshmallows. Using the uncooked spaghetti noodles and your strip of tape, work together to build the tallest tower you can. But being the tallest isn't the only thing you need to be concerned with. You also want to make your tower strong enough to support the weight of three marshmallows. Whoever has the tallest tower that can also support the weight of three marshmallows without falling is the winner!

....

....

....

....

....

....

....

....

....

....

....

....

Where Can I
Go From Your Spirit?

Scripture

Psalm 139:7–8

⁷ *I can never escape from your Spirit! I can never get away from your presence!* ⁸ *If I go up to heaven, you are there; if I go down to the grave, you are there.*

Windows Down (Taylor)

Logan's wife, Emily, didn't grow up in a typical Christian home. It wasn't that she was raised to disbelieve; there just wasn't much of a focus put on the things of God. Church attendance, Bible studies, or church youth group gatherings weren't regular occurrences for Emily. She was a remarkable student and a remarkable athlete, and she poured herself completely into those things. But as she poured herself out, as opposed to feeling fulfilled, she felt empty. There was a void in her life that she couldn't quite put her finger on, so she searched for the "thing" that would make her finally feel at peace. When that void wasn't fulfilled by academics or sports, she turned to a bottle of alcohol for the first time, she was twelve years old. The alcohol would help make the discomfort of her ongoing search for fulfillment and acceptance quiet down, but that discomfort would inevitably return every time.

This pattern of feeling something missing from her life but then turning to alcohol to numb that feeling continued for years. It followed her to college, and then into adulthood. She left home and moved to new cities, but everywhere she went, this pattern tagged along. She soon realized that alcohol was something that she didn't have control over. It was part of her everyday life. It was controlling her thoughts, her behavior, and her schedule. She didn't want this dependency on alcohol, but she didn't know how to break out of the cycle. At the peak of her struggle, it was alcohol that put Emily in the back of an ambulance, fighting for her life.

She had hit rock bottom. Emily was finally ready to get serious and admit she needed help. She needed saving. She had Christian people in her life who had talked about a loving God, a God that helped fight their battles, a God that transformed their hearts and minds. But she never knew if a God like that would be a God for *her*. It seemed to her that she'd gone too far, and that God was too good or holy to take time with someone like her. Either way, she didn't even know where to start when it came to God. After she was released from the hospital, she drove down the road. Thoughts of God were racing through her mind. She had so many questions, she had so many doubts, but in a fit of desperation she let out a simple prayer for help. "God, if you're real, I need you. I need you to show me." Thankfully, we have a God who answers beautiful, simple prayers just like that one.

As the words left her lips, the presence of God filled the car. She felt a warmth, a love, and a peace like she had never experienced. She felt the void in her heart and life being filled in that moment by the One who created her. She was so overcome that she pulled her car to the side of the road. At that very instant, the old had gone and the new had come. Emily made Jesus the Lord of her life that day. She committed herself to following Him, and He gave her new desires for her life. For the first time ever, she longed for the things of God. She longed to learn more about Him and to dive into godly community. She also wanted alcohol completely out of her life. She was able to get the support and resources she needed, and God paved the way for her to walk in sobriety for good.

Ever since that simple prayer while driving down the road, Emily's life has been completely transformed. She's sober, she's happily married, she's the mother of two beautiful daughters, and she's fulfilled. The void in her heart is now and forever completely satisfied by the love of Jesus. Even on her darkest day, she couldn't escape God's presence, as the psalmist wrote in Psalm 139. The Lord sought her out, found her right where she was, and brought her home to a relationship with Him.

Reflection Questions

- *Have you ever had a time where you felt like Emily in her story, that there was a void in your heart or something missing in your life?*
- *Jesus told the parable about the shepherd leaving his ninety-nine other sheep to save one that had gone astray. What do you think Jesus was trying to explain through this parable? Do you see yourself in that parable? If yes, how so?*

Activity

This one will take some slight preparation from the parents! Get a one-hundred-piece puzzle, and then secretly remove one piece and hide it somewhere in your home. Have the family work on this puzzle together. When the family discovers that one piece is missing, let them in on the secret that the final piece is hidden somewhere in the house. You can give them clues to where it is hidden, or you can tell them "warmer / colder" as they look around the house. Once the piece is found, complete the puzzle!

....

....

....

....

....

....

....

....

....

....

....

....

Praising on the Mountaintop

Scripture

Matthew 5:14-16

[14] *"You are the light of the world—like a city on a hilltop that cannot be hidden.* [15] *No one lights a lamp and then puts it under a basket. Instead, a lamp is placed on a stand, where it gives light to everyone in the house.* [16] *In the same way, let your good deeds shine out for all to see, so that everyone will praise your heavenly Father."*

Steven's Record-Setting Day (Logan)

There are nearly eight billion people on Earth. Of that massive number, only 949 are current players in Major League Baseball.[1] That means a mere one in ten million people are part of this elite group of athletes. Taylor's husband, Steven Matz, is one of them.

Hailing from Long Island, New York, the tall, hard-throwing left-hander was made to pitch a baseball. He has a fastball that can top 97 mph and a curveball that makes even the best hitters in the league look foolish. But getting to this level certainly

---

1   As of July 2024. See "Number of players on Major League Baseball rosters on opening day from 2013 to 2024," Statista, https://www.statista.com/ statistics/639334/major-league-baseball-players-on-opering-day-rosters/.

didn't come easy for Steven, and it didn't come overnight. After being drafted by the New York Mets in 2009, the work truly began. Steven worked his way up from a developmental rookie baseball league in the Dominican Republic all the way through the various levels of the Mets minor league baseball system. He battled injuries and withstood multiple throwing-arm surgeries. He wrestled with the fear and doubt that he would ever make it all the way to the Major Leagues. But through the fears, through the grueling workouts, Steven found strength in his relationship with Jesus.

Steven had come to faith during a tougher time in his rise through the minor leagues. He had injured his throwing arm and was recovering from surgery. Because his identity up to that point had been that of a baseball player, it was a crushing experience when he was unable to play. Steven eventually found himself at his rock bottom—mentally, physically, and emotionally. It was then that he was invited to a Bible study and thought to himself, *What do I have to lose?* Turns out, he had everything *to gain.* The Bible study lit a fire in the inquisitive Steven. He pored over the Word of God and soaked up as much teaching as he could. Steven gave his life to the Lord and was eager to share about the hope he had found. No longer was his identity found in baseball; it was found in Jesus. The ups and downs of his baseball career would inevitably come, but his purpose and mission were now set in stone: to tell the world about Jesus and glorify God in all that he did.

Finally, after six years of tireless work and preparation, Steven got the call that he was being brought up to the big leagues and would join the team in New York. His eyes were wide as he took in the sight of his first big-league clubhouse, and they became even wider when he stepped out onto the field for the first time with thousands of fans cheering in the stadium.

As Steven walked to the mound for his first appearance in a game, the moment felt absolutely surreal. He gripped the baseball tightly in his glove and took a deep breath as he stepped onto the pitching rubber. Before he could let any fear creep in, he settled himself with one thought. *Whether I win or lose on the field today, God is with me, and that is all that matters.*

And God was with him. Steven shook off any nerves and simply had a blast playing baseball that day. He proceeded to have an epic Major League debut, pitching nearly eight innings while only giving up two runs and striking out six batters. And if a dazzling pitching performance wasn't enough, Steven made history by getting three hits of his own and driving in four runs at the plate, which is still the most RBI for a pitcher and a member of the Mets in their Major League debut.

After the game, Steven was mobbed by sports reporters and fans asking for his take on his debut. Anyone and everyone couldn't wait to talk to the hometown hero and celebrate his historic day. But on the mountaintop of this great achievement, Steven chose to be, as the scriptures say, a city set upon a hill. He took the opportunity to shine brightly and proclaim his Savior's goodness proudly. Ultimately, Steven's response was the same as it was when he was in the valley of disappointment recovering from surgery: all glory, honor, and thanks belonged to God.

Reflection Questions

- *Today's scripture says to "let your light shine" before men. What do you think that means?*
- *What is the platform God has given you—a career, a school, a sports team, etc.? How can you use your platform to give honor and glory to God?*
- *Do you think it's harder to glorify God in the valleys of life or while on the mountaintops? Have you ever become too distracted to think about God when all things are going right?*

Activity

In honor of Steven, we're playing some indoor baseball today! All you'll need is either a paper towel roll (or the long tube from gift-wrapping paper) and an air-filled balloon. Pick four pieces of furniture to serve as the four bases, and you're ready to play. Have one person stand in the center and be the pitcher, and give the roll or tube to someone to be the batter. The first team to score five runs wins. PLAY BALL!

....
....
....
....
....
....
....

Give It to God

Scripture

Proverbs 19:21 ESV

²¹ *Many are the plans in the mind of a man, but it is the purpose of the Lord that will stand.*

Romans 8:28 KJV

²⁸ *And we know that all things work together for good to them that love God, to them who are the called according to his purpose.*

Hey, Jesus . . . (Taylor)

The typical career in the world of country music only lasts five years. For our band, after *over* five years of struggling to make it in the country music industry, we were no closer to becoming country music stars than when we began. We wasted nights performing in smoky barrooms across the country, we sunk every dollar we had into funding our own album, and we found ourselves at the end of our rope. In the years spent pursuing our dream, our lives had become more of a nightmare. We felt lost—without purpose. We felt depressed and anxious, and we had no meaningful friendships in our lives. How could a trio of typically joyful, bubbly pastor's kids fall to this new low? Ultimately, enough was enough—it was time to quit.

We knew it was time to make a change. So we decided to stop music altogether and return to the place that had defined our lives and our upbringing—*the church*. On our first Sunday back, we were instantly reminded of what we had been missing all along. The encouragement we experienced gathering with other believers was like a sip of cool water on a hot summer day. We worshipped our Savior with tears in our eyes, and we were so grateful to be in this uplifting environment. This was the most joyful we three had been in a long time.

After our first Sunday, we dived headlong into our new church home. We served as church greeters and members of the church café team. We led small groups in our homes and established deep friendships and community. Then, out of the blue, the need arose for us to help with the church worship team. We hadn't thought about music in quite some time, but we reluctantly said yes. When we played our first chords on that small church stage, for the first time in years, we found joy in music. The congregation lifted their voices worshipping Jesus, and we could hardly contain our emotions. The peace and happiness was unlike any we had experienced prior. Why? Because we were *finally* using the gifts God had given us for the *purpose* for which we were called. It was settled there and then. If music would ever be part of our lives again, it could only be about glorifying the name of Jesus.

We led our church family faithfully in worship week in and week out. Our love for music flourished now that it centered on praising God and helping others experience His presence. With our new sense of calm and gratefulness, we decided to sit down together and attempt to write a song again. We hadn't tried since we were writing country music, so our nerves were certainly present. But this time, before we strummed a guitar or drafted a lyric, we prayed to the Lord and thanked Him for how He'd brought our lives up from the ashes. We asked the Lord to speak to us and give us the lyric ideas to write, and that's exactly what He did. As we wrote the first lines of this new song, we wept tears of joy. A joy that we had never experienced washed over us as we penned words about the goodness of our God.

After this day, the Lord laid more and more songs on our hearts. He opened doors of opportunity for our band to sing about Jesus all over the country. But now, instead of seeking stardom or striving to make a name for ourselves, we seek to bring glory and honor to the God that pulled us up out of the pit and gave us a purpose.

Our story has a simple but life-challenging message: When you give your gifts, your talents, and your dreams over to God, He will do exceedingly more than you could ever imagine. He will establish your steps, and He will help guide you into more joy than you will ever find on your own.

Reflection Questions

- *The first of today's scriptures says many are the plans of a man, but the Lord's purpose will stand. Parents, share with your kids about a time that you had big plans, but ultimately God had something else in mind for you. How was God's plan far better than yours?*
- *What feelings do you experience when you think about handing over your dreams and desires to the Lord?*

- *What is a tangible way you can use your gifts and talents for God's purposes instead of just your own?*

Activity

It's Family Vision Board time! Supplies: old magazines or newspapers, scissors, glue or glue sticks, and a poster board. A Vision Board is a collage of images and words that you should display in a prominent place to remind you why you do what you do every day; images and words that spark your motivation and remind you of your values, goals, or dreams. It could also be filled with things that inspire you or leave you feeling happy.

Take the time to look through the magazines and newspapers and cut out the images and words that make you smile, feel motivated, or get inspired. Glue those images to the poster board. Once it dries, have each family member share what they put on their Vision Board and what each image or word means to them.

....

....

....

....

....

....

....

....

Ill-Gotten Treasures

Scripture

1 John 1:9

⁹ *But if we confess our sins to him, he is faithful and just to forgive us our sins and to cleanse us from all wickedness.*

Proverbs 10:2 NIV

² *Ill-gotten treasures have no lasting value, but righteousness delivers from death.*

The Offering Bandits (Logan)

Growing up as pastor's kids gave us a deep familiarity with the church. Every time the door was open—*we were there.* From birth, we could be found each Sunday on the front row watching our dad deliver a powerful message from God's Word, and we even spent most of our weekdays in the church building. But even with that much exposure to the house of God, kids will be kids from time to time.

When Taylor and Madison were seven and six years old, respectively, they were spending a weekday entertaining themselves in the church while our parents worked on important church business. On this day, however, it was particularly difficult for the girls to play when they kept catching glimpses of the new soda vending machine that had been installed in the church kitchenette. Each time the girls ran through the auditorium, they'd notice this glorious machine in all its sugary soda goodness. When you're seven and six, you often don't have money to spend at a vending machine. But on this fateful day, the girls hatched a great (terrible) idea.

While playing in the church secretary's office, the girls noticed a large number of coins organized neatly on the secretary's desk. "That's it," exclaimed Taylor. "We can use these quarters to get a soda out of the vending machine!" Being that she was six, Madison bought into our sister's plan instantly. Their childhood logic seemed airtight to both of them, and there was more than enough coinage for both of them to have a soda. It made perfect sense!

The girls approached a stack of quarters and each pulled out $0.50. Then they quickly made their way back to the vending machine and helped themselves to an ice-cold soda. They knew their idea had worked perfectly, but what they *didn't* know was that they'd received their $0.50 courtesy of the church's tithes and offerings. The coins had been counted and organized on the secretary's desk only to be taken to the bank later that day for deposit. But to the girls, they were just quarters free to use as anyone had need . . . and they had *need* for a Coke. The duo walked proudly upstairs to our dad's office with their brightly colored soda cans gleaming in their hands. When Dad raised his head from his work, the site of the cans made his eyes open wide.

Parents have a knack for knowing when their kids have misbe-haved, and our dad was no different. He knew his daughters didn't arrive at church that morning with loose change jingling in their pockets, and he also knew they didn't ask him for any quarters to buy a soda. So he quickly came to the realization that his precious daughters must have come up with their own scheme. He stood from his desk and approached them with a simple question. "Hey girls, where did you get the money to buy those sodas?"

"Oh, we just got the quarters off of the secretary's desk," beamed Taylor as she took another sip of her soda. Taylor and Madison's smiles quickly faded when they saw our father didn't have *quite* the same level of excitement at their creative thinking skills as they did. To their surprise, our dad had the opposite reaction! They couldn't believe it. The best idea they *ever* had was about to get them in the most *trouble* they'd ever been in. As calmly, but sternly, as possible, Dad explained to the girls that those quarters were part of the church's tithes and offerings and that they were *not* for free use at a vending machine. While he understood this was an innocent mistake, he took the opportunity to explain to the girls the purpose of tithing and why these quarters were so important. Taylor and Madison understood, and they apologized for what they had done.

As they turned to leave our dad's office, they were surprised their punishment hadn't been more severe. They exchanged glances of relief as they exited. Just as they each went to take a final sip of their sodas, Dad stuck his head out of his office door and added, "Oh, and by the way, to make amends for taking this money, you'll each have to pay back seven times what you took . . . $3.50 each. You can earn some of that right now by going to sweep the church auditorium."

That was the last time Taylor or Madison ever purchased a soda with anything other than their own money, and ultimately, they learned that their ill-gotten "treasures" didn't taste quite as sweet as treasures earned rightfully. Above all else, they learned that if and when they made a mistake, it was always best to confess it all the way, right away!

Reflection Questions

- *Parents, share with your kids a time when you made an innocent mistake as a child. What happened, and did you suffer any consequences?*
- *Today's scripture says when we confess our sins to God, He is faithful to forgive us, yet sometimes we have trouble believing this. What keeps you from believing God will forgive you?*
- *The scripture also says that ill-gotten treasures have no lasting value. Was there ever a time you received an "ill-gotten treasure"? Was this treasure as rewarding as treasure received from honest, hard work?*

Activity

Sweet Detectives—A Game on Honesty! Set out a variety of treats on the kitchen table (marshmallows, cake icing, pudding, cookie crumbs, chocolate chips, etc.). Have all but one person exit the room. The person left in the kitchen may sample one of the treats. (With younger kids, make sure an adult stays back to supervise quantities). When the person has sampled one of the treats, that person calls everyone else back into the kitchen. Invite the others to inspect the treats to try and guess which treat has been sampled. Make note of any deceptions that the "sampler" may have used such as spilling extra crumbs on the table to make the others believe they actually sampled that treat. As a group, guess which treat was sampled. Take turns until everyone has had the chance to be the sampler at least once.

Know That You Know

Scripture
Romans 10:9-13 NIV

⁹ If you declare with your mouth, "Jesus is Lord," and believe in your heart that God raised him from the dead, you will be saved. ¹⁰ For it is with your heart that you believe and are justified, and it is with your mouth that you profess your faith and are saved. ¹¹ As Scripture says, "Anyone who believes in him will never be put to shame."¹² For there is no difference between Jew and Gentile—the same Lord is Lord of all and richly blesses all who call on him, ¹³ for, "Everyone who calls on the name of the Lord will be saved."

Let's Settle This Right Now . . . (Taylor)

Madison's husband, Jared, grew up in a Christian home. He and his family attended a Southern Baptist church every Sunday, he took part in vacation Bible school in the summers, and he would even attend Royal Ambassador meetings at church on Wednesday nights. Yet with all this time spent in God's house, the true meaning of the gospel didn't take root for Jared until later in life. His understanding of God's love and mercy was all based around one thing: himself and his conduct. If Jared behaved and studied his Bible, he felt in good standing with the Lord. He felt as though God's grace was meant for him. But if he misbehaved or went weeks without praying or studying God's Word, he felt that his good standing had changed. How could God's grace cover him if he made mistakes?

This roller-coaster pattern of thinking stuck with Jared through childhood and into his high school years. His walk with God ebbed and flowed and, whether he realized it or not, he placed the full responsibility of his salvation on his own shoulders. Then, in the summer of 2008, Jared was invited by his best friend, (our brother) Logan, to attend a youth group camp. Jared was ready for more in his relationship with the Lord. He was ready for this up-and-down spiritual life to move to the "up" position . . . for good. The camp kicked off in typical youth group fashion where the attendees were placed into small groups to share their names, reveal a fun fact about themselves, and answer the infamous question, "What do you hope to get out of youth camp?" This may have seemed like a standard camp kickoff activity, but the Lord had a life-changing plan in place for Jared.

The leader of Jared's small group was our dad, Pastor Charley Cain, and thankfully for Jared, Dad didn't waste time with pleasantries. "Jared, what do you hope to get out of camp?" he asked. The abruptness of the question caught Jared off guard, but with little time to think, he answered truthfully. "I guess I just want to *know* that I'm saved. I have times when I feel close to God, but inevitably I mess up. Eventually, I neglect God. I just worry that I've let God down too many times for this to ever 'stick' for me."

The raw honesty of his answer startled Jared, but he felt relief finally saying this thought out loud. In his typical fashion, Pastor

Charley wasted no time with what to do next. "Jared, buddy, you *can't* let God down. You can't let Him down because you aren't even the one holding Him up! He's holding *you* up." He added, "He is your Savior and friend. And His word says that whoever calls upon the name of the Lord will be saved—right then and there— for good."

The truth has a ring to it, and the simple truth spoken by Pastor Charley wrapped around Jared's heart like a warm blanket. He felt a peace and assurance for which he had been longing. "If you're ready, let's handle this right now," Dad continued. Then, like the loving pastor and father he is, he draped his arm around Jared's shoulder and led him in calling upon the name of the Lord through the Sinner's Prayer. And with their final *amen,* Jared's life was changed. He finally realized his standing with God and his salvation weren't reliant on himself. By God's grace he had been saved, and God's grace did not run out and would never stop applying to Jared as long as he lived.

Reflection Questions

- *Have you ever felt like Jared did, like you've let God down?*
- *Today's scripture says God's mercies are made new every morning. How does that make you feel? Is that sometimes difficult to believe?*
- *How would your relationship with God change if you whole-heartedly believed His grace was sufficient for you?*

Activity

Holding You Up: This game requires five people and one chair. Have one person sit in the chair. Then have the other four people stand around the seated person and clasp their hands together with their two index fingers pointed out (this will make their hands appear like a pistol). Then the four people should put their index fingers underneath the seated person's arm and knee pits and try to lift them into the air. It should prove to be very difficult. Next, have the four standing people all place their hands on top of the seated person's head. Then count down from three to zero and try to lift the seated person in the same way as before. This time, with everyone lifting simultaneously, they should be able to lift the seated person! Take turns lifting one another.

....

....

....

....

....

....

....

....

....

....

Keep Your Cool

Scripture

Proverbs 14:29

29 *People with understanding control their anger; a hot temper shows great foolishness.*

Proverbs 16:32 NKJV

32 *He who is slow to anger is better than the mighty, And he who rules his spirit than he who takes a city.*

A Relaxing Day on the Course (Logan)

When asked about the mental toughness required to play the game of golf, professional golfer Percy Boomer said, "If you wish to hide your character, do not play golf."[2] In my time on a golf course, this has proven to be incredibly true. It is wild how this tiny white, dimpled ball can cause me so much joy one moment and then searing frustration and anger the next. No matter the number of practice swings or YouTube lessons I take, I inevitably scatter a few mistakes throughout each round of golf I play. The key is to maintain composure when these periodic issues happen. However, when my brother-in-law Jared steps onto the

2   *On Learning Golf: A Valuable Guide to Better Golf* (Knopf, 1946), 219.

golf course, he experiences more of a series of golfing errors and calamities with a few periodic brilliant shots sprinkled in.

Because of his struggles on the course, Jared doesn't play golf with me very often. But one fateful day I finally convinced Jared and my dad, Charley, to join me for a casual eighteen holes. The round ended up being *anything* but casual. Each hole Jared would swing as hard as he could, and it was anyone's guess as to where each ball was going. He spent time digging golf balls out of the deep woods, fishing them out of the bottom of ponds, and growing more frustrated with each swing. Jared's a pretty mild-mannered guy, but even the most tender and mild golfers would be tested by the results Jared was seeing on the course that day. Thankfully, after hours of relentless struggle, we approached the final hole of the day—number eighteen.

Jared pulled his neon yellow driver from his bag and sheep-ishly approached the tee box. His hopes for the hole were notice-ably low as he muttered to himself and placed his golf ball on the tee. He settled into his stance, peered down the fairway toward the green, and began his backswing. Then, in a rare moment of mastery, Jared's swing aligned perfectly, and he hit the golf ball squarely on the nose! The ball launched off the tee and screamed through the air. My dad and stood there astonished, our mouths agape. "No way!" shouted Jared. He watched with great surprise as his golf ball soared through the air. On the last hole, no less, he'd finally hit the ball in the proper direction. The three of us celebrated together while the ball continued its flight. But then, the golf ball began to fade ever so slightly to the right.

The final hole of this golf course had a fairway that seemed a mile wide. It was a forgiving way to end even the most troublesome of rounds. There was nothing but well-cut grass between you and the green...apart from one lone oak tree. This mighty oak stood safely off the fairway, but on this day, one pesky branch hung out into the field of play. The odds that a tiny golf ball hits an equally tiny tree branch in a wide-open fairway are slim, but Jared's magnificently struck ball defied the odds and smacked the tree branch squarely. I'd love to say that the golf ball snapped the tree branch and continued on its path, but no, it didn't. It fell immediately to the ground far shy of the green. You could hear a pin drop among us as we looked on, silently stunned. In that moment, I turned my head back to check on Jared. I expected him to be hurling his club deep into the forest or maybe even pushing the golf cart into the pond, but that wasn't the case—he was laughing.

"Well, I couldn't do that again if I tried," Jared chuckled. He added, "Man, I *really* got ahold of that one." Seeing Jared laugh at himself gave us the permission to laugh along with him. We laughed for the rest of the final hole and then the whole way home. Then we laughed even more when we retold the story of the lone, rogue tree branch to the rest of our family. We have gotten more enjoyment retelling that story than we ever have recounting a perfectly executed golf shot.

Jared understood that, as today's scripture says, there is no value in showing a hot temper. By being slow to anger and controlling his spirit, he made himself not only more like our Savior, but also way more fun to be around in life and on the golf course!

Reflection Questions

- *Share a time when your temper got the better of you. What happened? How did you feel afterward?*
- *The scripture says he who is slow to anger is better than the mighty. What are some practical ways you can be slow to anger?*
- *Take the time to pray together as a family. Thank God that He is slow to anger and abounding in love for you all. Ask the Lord to help you be like Him, slow to anger with one another and with everyone you encounter each day.*

Activity

Homemade Mini Golf: Let's see if you can have better luck than Jared. All you'll need is a golf ball (or other similar-sized ball), a makeshift golf club (an umbrella or yardstick would do nicely), and a drinking cup. Lay the drinking cup on the ground and take turns using the makeshift golf club to tap the ball into the cup. You can set up obstacles and create difficult angles to make your putts more challenging. Play nine holes and keep track of how many strokes it takes you to hit the ball into the cup. The lowest number of strokes after nine holes wins!

Memorial Stones

Scripture

Joshua 4:5–7

[5] *He told them, "Go into the middle of the Jordan, in front of the Ark of the Lord your God. Each of you must pick up one stone and carry it out on your shoulder—twelve stones in all, one for each of the twelve tribes of Israel.* [6] *We will use these stones to build a memorial. In the future your children will ask you, 'What do these stones mean?'* [7] *Then you can tell them, 'They remind us that the Jordan River stopped flowing when the Ark of the Lord's Covenant went across.' These stones will stand as a memorial among the people of Israel forever."*

That Old Piano (Logan)

A love for music was instilled in us at a very early age. If you stuck your ear to the door of our childhood home, you'd hear us running around singing "The Great Adventure" by the great Steven Curtis Chapman at the tops of our tiny lungs. Our dad was (and still is) an incredible worship leader, and by the time we could walk he was putting instruments in our hands. And there was no instrument more impactful than our family's old stand-up piano.

Taylor, the oldest of us kids, took to this whole music thing rather quickly. She had perfect singing pitch even as a child, she came up with her own unique melodies, and there is even home video footage of four-year-old Taylor trying to teach three-year-old Madison how to harmonize.

One day while our father was at work, four-year-old Taylor felt rather inspired by a little tune that Dad had taught her. So she climbed up the bench nestled under the family piano and uncovered the keys. Key by key, Taylor slowly but surely found all the right notes for that little song. Before you knew it, she could play the tune with ease—she was a regular Mozart! She was so proud of herself and could not wait to show her new skills to our dad once he got home, but she feared by the time he arrived that she would forget the right notes to play.

Quickly, Taylor descended the piano bench and went to find scratch paper and a pen to write down the sequence of notes, but there was none to be found. Normally, this would deter most children, but most children aren't like Taylor Cain. She went to the silverware drawer and pulled out a butter knife. Then, without alerting our mother, Taylor returned to the family piano, and using the butter knife, carved the notes to this little song into the wooden, front face of the piano. "There! Now I won't forget it," Taylor said as she sat back and admired her work.

Now, our dad *was* surprised to say the least when he returned home and saw the crude carvings on the front of the piano. And sure, young Taylor received a talking to about not carving letters into family instruments. But Dad couldn't help but be filled with joy because of his children's love for music. Those simple carved letters remained on the piano for as long as it sat in our family's first home. And each time anyone asked about those markings, it served as a reminder that our deep love for music and music skills were gifts from God. Those scrawled letters gave our parents a deep knowing that whatever plan the Lord was laying before us would undoubtedly involve music.

Years later, we moved into a new home and the old, family piano (carved letters and all) had to be rehomed to a new family. We greatly missed it, but the story of tiny Taylor and her handy dandy butter knife lived on. With each telling of the story, we were all reminded that this desire to make music was not just an infatuation but a calling for us three. As time passed, the Lord steadily led us on a journey to make music for Him—a journey to encourage a broken and hurting world with songs of hope and truth.

The Lord does have a sense of humor, however. After decades of absence, we found our old family piano. It had been passed to multiple new owners but was still residing in our hometown. So as adults, we were reunited with this beautiful family treasure and brought it home for good. Even after all these years, Taylor's carved letters still show proudly across the piano's front—a memorial stone of all the powerful things that God had done.

Reflection Questions

- *Read the story of Joshua 3 where the Israelites crossed the Jordan River on dry ground. Why did God instruct Joshua to make the stone memorial in Joshua 4?*
- *Are there any memorial stones among your family that remind you of God's faithfulness?*

- *What could your family establish today that could serve as a memorial stone that makes you consider the Lord every time you see it?*

....

....

....

....

....

....

....

....

....

....

See Something, Do Something

Scripture

1 John 3:18 ESV

¹⁸ *Little children, let us not love in word or talk but in deed and in truth.*

James 4:17 ESV

¹⁷ *So whoever knows the right thing to do and fails to do it, for him it is sin.*

Smash Cake (Jared)

It was a particularly crazy day at our home. Madison and I scurried around our house making final preparations for our son Calloway's joint first birthday party with his cousin Stevie. While we were making multiple trips to the car lugging party supplies, little Cal sat quietly in his high chair enjoying a nice little snack of milk and colorful veggie chips. Calloway and his high chair were the two final things to be loaded up before we left for the party, so when the time came, I made my way over to Cal to remove the food tray and unbuckle him. But on this day, the food tray wouldn't budge. I pulled and pulled yet couldn't get it free. On a normal, calm day, I would have taken an extra second to diagnose the problem and remove the tray carefully. But because I was in a rush, I strained with the high chair's tray like a frustrated ape. Then I exacted every ounce of my strength onto the white, plastic IKEA high chair food tray and *broke* the pesky tray off.

Based on the sound that it made, I knew I might have damaged it. Sure enough, two very small (but vital) plastic tabs were snapped off of the food tray. These plastic tabs helped secure the tray to the high chair. I quickly reinstalled the food tray and gave it a strength test. For the most part, it worked fine. But if just the right amount of downward pressure was applied, it would fall off of the high chair entirely and onto the floor. Again, on a normal day I would have decommissioned this chair until the tray was repaired. But on *this* day, I loaded the damaged high chair into the car, hoped for the best, and headed to the party.

The birthday party went swimmingly. Calloway and Stevie enjoyed their cowboy-themed decorations and party treats. Sweet friends and family showered them with birthday gifts. Then it was time for the moment everyone was waiting for . . . the cake. It's a tradition for a child's first birthday to give them what is known as a "smash cake." You place a simple cake in front of the birthday boy or girl and allow them free rein. They tend to smack the cake, eat fistfuls of icing, and rub cake bits all through their hair. It's quite the sight, and finally it was Calloway's time to smash his cake. I placed Cal into his high chair and installed the damaged food tray. As I snapped the food tray weakly into place, I thought to myself, *I wonder if this tray is going to hold? Maybe we should find another high chair.* Before I could complete my internal dialogue, Madison entered the room with Calloway's beautiful smash cake and a smile from ear to ear.

It was like a slow-motion action movie sequence and I was stuck in quicksand. As the partygoers sang "Happy Birthday," Madison arrived at the high chair. She carefully placed the smash cake onto the chair's food tray while I tried to push through family members to stop her. Then like a flash of lighting, Calloway struck the smash cake with his hand with the strength of a toddler Bruce Lee. The food tray snapped like a feeble twig and the beautiful cake went barreling to the floor. Smash! Cake met hardwood floor and sent sweet shrapnel all over the room. The party guests all yelled in terror as Madison and I tried to scoop cake roadkill off the floor, but the deed was already done. The cake was smashed.

Cal won't remember his first birthday party at all, and he certainly won't remember the great cake drop. But this entire scenario could've been prevented if his well-meaning father would have spoken up, taken the extra time, and either fixed his high chair or removed it entirely from the equation. I knew what was right to do and failed to do it, and then my consequence came shortly thereafter! While it may have seemed like a small, delicious mistake, this was an important lesson that taking the extra time to do the right thing (even when you're rushing to set up a birthday party) is an important way to truly love those around you.

Reflection Questions

- *Have you ever been like Jared in this scenario? Have you known something was wrong but kept silent?*
- *Throughout his teachings, Jesus stressed that as believers we are to go the extra mile for others. What does that look like practically in your life? Who is someone at your office, school, or social circle you could go the extra mile for this week?*

- *Today's scripture says we aren't to love in word or talk but in deed, with our actions. Go around the table and share a time that you were shown love in action by one another.*

Activity

Love in Action: As a family, think of a way you can love one of your neighbors in deed and truth this week. You could complete a yard work or home improvement project for them, bake them cookies, or give them a gift. Put some thought into which neighbor to show love to and what you'd like to do as a family. Get out there and love in deed!

....
....
....
....
....
....
....
....
....
....
....
....

He's in the Details

Scripture

Luke 12:6–7 ESV

⁶ *"Are not five sparrows sold for two pennies? And not one of them is forgotten before God. ⁷ Why, even the hairs of your head are all numbered. Fear not; you are of more value than many sparrows."*

Matthew 6:26 NIV

²⁶ *"Look at the birds of the air; they do not sow or reap or store away in barns, and yet your heavenly Father feeds them. Are you not much more valuable than they?"*

Three Calls (Taylor)

From singing praises at iconic music venues like the Grand Ole Opry and Red Rocks Amphitheater to worshipping alongside our musical heroes like Steven Curtis Chapman and TobyMac, our music career has been an unbelievable adventure. But before there was anyone to listen to our songs or purchase a concert ticket, we already had our biggest fan—our mom. If you looked up the definition of a supportive, praying mother, there would likely be a photo of Shari Cain. No matter the concert, no matter the opportunity, Mom has been there covering us in prayer.

The touring lifestyle is one of constant change. Every day involves a new city, a new venue, and a new audience. But amid the change and uncertainty, there is always one constant for us. After each show, like clockwork, Mom will call and speak to all three of us. One by one, she will ask each of us about the show—how it went, how we felt, did we have a good time. You'd think after the first phone call, she'd lose steam, considering she would have heard all the details of the show, but to each of us she responds with the same excitement and enthusiasm as if she were hearing about it for the first time. Each of us feels like the most important person in the world during those phone calls. One time Logan asked our mom, "Wait, have you already heard about this from the girls?" To which she responded, "Well, yes. But I haven't heard about it from *your* perspective yet."

The beauty in these phone calls lies in one place—the details. By the time we hang up the phone, we know without a shadow of a doubt that our mother cares deeply about the small details of our lives. She listens earnestly, asks thoughtful questions, calmly encourages, and reminds us of what is true and lovely. She's never too busy to care. She's never too busy to offer her love and concern. And that, undoubtedly, mirrors the love of our heavenly Father.

Our God is so big and mighty, to the point that Scripture says that the nations are like "dust" on His measuring scales (Isaiah 40:15). Yet even with His might and His supremacy, our God chooses to know us intimately. The Bible paints the picture for us that we have a God who profoundly cares. He cares about our little worries, little prayers, and little disappointments. His Word even tells us that the hairs on our heads are numbered by God.

In a world full of confusion and unreliability, we can all be assured of one thing: our God *cares* for us. Like Shari Cain calling her three kids to hear three detailed perspectives, our God is there for us. He's there to listen, to point us back to the truth, and to extend to us the comfort of His presence. Thank goodness for mothers who call and for a God who cares.

Reflection Questions

- *The scripture in Matthew referenced above assures us about the level to which God cares for and values us. Have you ever had trouble feeling "valuable" to God? If so, why?*
- *God cares about even the small details of our lives. How would your prayer life change if you took hold of that fact?*
- *The love we receive from our family can mirror the love of our heavenly Father. Have you ever experienced this type of love where you knew someone cared deeply about the details of your life? Who was it? How did that make you feel?*

Activity

Telephone Game: Have your family sit in a circle. One person will start the game by whispering a funny phrase into the ear of the person next to them. Then that person will try to whisper the same phrase into the ear of the person seated next to them. Repeat this action until the whispered phrase reaches the last person in the circle. The last person will say the funny phrase aloud and everyone will see if it matches what was first whispered. Typically, key details and words are changed or forgotten from person to person. Try this for a few rounds and see if you can get the phrase repeated correctly at the end of the circle!

....
....
....
....
....
....
....
....
....
....
....
....

It Takes a Village

Scripture

Numbers 11:17

[17] *"They will bear the burden of the people along with you, so you will not have to carry it alone."*

River Runs Wild (Madison)

In March of 2022, the entire Cain family was forever changed when little River Cain entered the world. Logan and his wife, Emily, beamed with pride and gratefulness as they took in the sight of their beautiful baby girl, and what a sight she was. River was a *first* for everyone. She was the first grandchild for our mom and dad. She was the first child for any of the members of CAIN the band. And she was the first baby that many of us would spend considerable time around in general. Even so, once Logan and Emily made the safe and slow drive back home with their new bundle of joy, it was quickly apparent that raising a child would not be for the faint of heart.

The first few nights at home were likened to the days between Christmas and New Year's. No one could say confidently what day it was, what time it was, or when was the last time any of us showered. We were all up at odd hours of the night to help soothe

the baby, change diapers, clean bottles, whatever was needed to help. But it was in these sleep-deprived days that we all learned that the old adage, "It takes a village," was not only true regarding raising children but for our lives in general. In helping this infant, we became acutely aware that our own individual strength and ability would never be enough to meet *all* her needs *all* the time. If we didn't work together, pitch in, and lend a hand, we'd all wear down, and quickly.

This was truly a case in point for how God has called us to live our lives. We were made for relationship with one another. And through these relationships, we bear one another's burdens, and we serve one another to help carry the load of life. The Lord knew this when He came to Moses's aid in Numbers 11. Moses was frustrated, tired, and feeling alone in his mission to lead the Israelites to the Promised Land. The people of Israel continued to defy the Lord and make life increasingly difficult for Moses, but the Lord was delighted to help Moses when he finally asked for it.

The Lord helped Moses by providing *people*—people to help bear the burden so Moses wouldn't carry it alone. God uses the solution of *people* often in our lives: people to help us push our dead car to a service station, people with whom to share our emotional struggles, and lo and behold, people to help us raise our children. It's in our respective "villages" that God helps us accomplish more than we would ever accomplish by ourselves.

We've continued this "it takes a village" approach as our family grows. We're up to four CAIN the band babies now; we're quickly becoming outnumbered by tiny humans. But in the growth, the stretching, and the trying, we can take heart and know that at any given moment, our village is ready to rise up and help whoever is

in need. If ever we are weak, He is strong. And if ever we feel helpless, He is faithful to send *helpers.*

Reflection Questions

- *Parents, share a specific time you realized you needed a
  "village" when raising your kids.*
- *How is one way your family works well together? Where is an
  area that you all can improve?*
- *Are you currently carrying a burden that your family can
  come alongside you and help with? If so, share with your
  family, pray together, and put a plan in place to help one
  another.*

Activity

*Stand Up! This quick activity demonstrates how working
together can help us accomplish difficult tasks. First, have
everyone sit on the floor. Don't sit crisscross applesauce but sit
with your knees folded to the height of your chest. Without using
your hands, attempt to stand up from this seated position. Some
of you may be able to accomplish it on your own, but most will
struggle! Next, sit back-to-back with another family member in
the same fashion. Now you and your family member attempt
to stand up, still without using your hands. But you may press
your back into your family member's back for support. When
you work with another person, you'll see it's much easier to
stand to your feet. Give it a try!*

A Lasting Impact

Scripture

Psalm 37:4-5

[4] *Take delight in the Lord, and he will give you your heart's desires.*

5 *Commit everything you do to the Lord. Trust him, and he will help you.*

IAM4KIDS (Logan)

In the little town of Loretto, Tennessee, there aren't many people who don't know the name Theresa Beck. Theresa is a founder and president of a local children's ministry that has greatly impacted the charming southern town. She was even the recipient of a Governor's Volunteer Star Award. But to CAIN the band, Theresa Beck is best known as "Nana." We may be leading people in worship all across the country, but our ministry involvement is simply the continuation of a legacy started by our grandmother.

In the summer of 1996, Nana was leading a weekly Bible study for the women of a local Methodist church. She had grown up in this small town, and over time, the neighborhood surrounding this church had changed. More and more children lived in this area, and during the summers with nothing else to do, they would gather in the church parking lot to play and maybe even get into a little mischief. Each day that Nana would arrive at the church to lead her Bible study, she would see these children huddled together in the parking lot, and she would feel a tug on her heart. She couldn't explain it, but she felt a connection to these kids and wondered if there was a way she could help them. Little did she know the Lord was preparing her heart for something far greater than she could imagine—and it all began with one little girl.

As Nana was grabbing her Bible and notebook out of her back seat, a child broke away from the pack and approached her with a simple request. "What are y'all doing in there? Can I come?" At first Nana was taken aback by the question, surprised that this young girl would have any interest in a women's Bible study. But then the Holy Spirit placed a simple yet powerful idea into her mind. She replied, "I tell you what. You likely won't have too much fun in there; it's just a bunch of older ladies. But I promise, we can have our own meeting next week and I'll be sure to bring snacks!" Nana held to her promise. She showed up early to her Bible study meeting the next week with a snack to share. To her surprise, that little girl was there but wasn't alone; she had invited several other children to join her.

This started a weekly trend. Nana would show up early to her Bible study, snacks in tow, and each week more and more children would come and meet with her. They would sit together under a big shade tree, enjoy their snacks, and laugh and talk about the *big* happenings in the life of a child. Soon, these moments of connection opened the door for Nana to share why she was coming to the church in the first place—*Jesus*. Each week, the kids would have a slew of questions about Jesus, the Bible, and heaven. Their minds were abuzz with curiosity, and they could hardly wait to learn more.

Nana wanted to go about this in the right way, so she went door-to-door in the neighborhood to speak to the parents of these children. She was up-front and shared with the parents what she was doing. "I'm here to help your kids, give them a snack, and teach them about Jesus." The parents all responded positively; they could tell how much Nana valued their children. And with the parents' blessing, Nana's ministry for children was born. What started humbly in a church parking lot grew. Soon it morphed into an after-school meeting each week at a local elementary school. More and more children would show up to hear a gospel message, play games, and of course, enjoy a snack. Local churches joined in until hundreds of elementary-aged children were being positively affected each week. In her second year of holding these meetings, Nana was invited to start an afternoon program for older students as well, and before too long, there were *two* Christ-centered after-school programs where students could hear the gospel and have their bodies and spirits fed.

It's now been twenty-eight years, and what started simply as a tug on Nana's heart has grown into an after-school mentoring program known as IAM4KIDS, the "I AM" standing for the Great I Am, our heavenly Father. School and faith communities all over the state and country have replicated Nana's approach, but even with this recognition and longevity, her heart has remained the same. "You know, I just made it up as I went along," she told us. "God put a simple desire in my heart, and then through the body of Christ—the schools, teachers, churches, courts, police—God used *all* of His body to make it happen. He did far more than I could have ever dreamed. All I had to do was trust Him."

Reflection Questions

- *Today's scripture tells us that as we delight in the Lord, He gives us the desires of our hearts. What has been a desire of your heart that you feel is from God? Do you have a heart for ministry, for art, for music—what is it for you?*
- *What is a practical way you can commit a desire of your heart to the Lord? For example, if you love sports, what is a way you can commit that to the Lord and honor Him through it?*
- *Do you have someone in your family who has left a legacy of following Jesus like Nana? Who is that person, and how have they impacted you?*

Activity

In honor of CAIN's Nana, kick it back to the roots of her IAM4KIDS ministry. Take your family Bible outside (and a snack!). Find you a nice shady spot to sit down and enjoy your snack together while you read all of Psalm 37 as a family. After you read, discuss your favorite parts of the passage and what it means to you.

....

....

....

....

....

....

Though I Walk through the Valley

Scripture

Psalm 23

[1] *The Lord is my shepherd; I have all that I need.* [2] *He lets me rest in green meadows; he leads me beside peaceful streams.* [3] *He renews my strength. He guides me along right paths, bringing honor to his name.* [4] *Even when I walk through the darkest valley, I will not be afraid, for you are close beside me. Your rod and your staff protect and comfort me.* [5] *You prepare a feast for me in the presence of my enemies. You honor me by anointing my head with oil. My cup overflows with blessings.* [6] *Surely your goodness and unfailing love will pursue me all the days of my life, and I will live in the house of the Lord forever.*

Public School Nightmare (Logan)

In a small southern hometown with only one city school system, the decision to homeschool us was an uncommon choice for our mom and dad. They wanted the best education possible for us three, but before we entered the world on our own and had our *peers* try to tell us who we were, they wanted us to be assured of our identity in Jesus. So for years we were homeschooled, and we loved every minute of the family time and free-learning style it provided. But once Taylor reached the age to attend ninth grade at the local public high school, the family came together and made the decision that it was time for all of us Cain kids to make the leap to public school. In one day, we would start ninth, eighth, and seven grade, respectively.

As Dad pulled up to the school on the first day, he threw his old Chevy Tahoe into park and turned to address us all. "You're going to do great," he said. "But the first day can be tough. Try to give it a week. If you hate it, and still hate it after a week, I'll bring you right back home." With both our father's vote of confidence and his option for a fallback plan, we each took a deep breath and walked into our new schools. Within minutes, it was clear we weren't ready for this.

Watching kids' television shows set in school hardly prepared a homeschool kid to take on an actual public school. On TV, the school bell would ring, and the main character would say something cool like "got to jet to class" before skating away on their skateboard. (Cue laugh track.) But in real-life public school, you were supposed to be in your classroom and seated at your desk when the bell rang, or else you were considered "late for class." Also on TV, nothing seemed more fun than spending time at your locker between classes, but what they should have done is given the viewer a full tutorial on how to use a combination lock. Because for a bewildered homeschool kid, a tricky combo lock might as well have been a Rubik's Cube. If there was a logistical issue to encounter on a first day, we experienced it. But the logistical issues were just the tip of the iceberg.

During Taylor's first day at the high school, she heard language in the hallways that would make most sailors blush. It was certainly not how our parents spoke at home. For Madison, she encountered some rather crude eighth-grade boys who desperately wanted attention. Again, a far cry from how things were at home. And for me ... well, I happened to cause more trouble than experience it at the hands of someone else. In my first week of middle school, I ended up in the principal's office after some new friends and I "borrowed" Axe body spray out of another student's gym locker. The punishment of smelling like sweaty seventh-grade boys doused with Axe body spray nearly fit the crime.

Needless to say, the blend of culture shock, unsavory encounters, and out-of-character behaviors made this new experience rather difficult. But it was in this moment of challenge that we harkened back to the teachings we'd received at home. We knew we were called to be a light in the darkness, a city on a hill for our fellow classmates. We knew that, though we were walking into a new and intimidating place, God was always with us and going before us.

So we decided to keep showing up even when it was tough. We resolved to see what would happen if we allowed the Lord to truly be our shepherd in what seemed like a scary situation. Day by day, the Lord continually proved He was very much good and present. He renewed our strength each moment as we eventually mastered our lockers and school schedules. He led us beside peaceful streams as He brought meaningful friendships into our lives. He guided us successfully through our first year of public school, and that set the table for any challenges and tough times that followed.

When all seems lost, and you find yourself with nowhere to turn, the Lord is there, like a good shepherd, to protect and comfort us until our lives overflow with His blessings.

Reflection Questions

- *Have you ever had an intimidating first day of school or even a new job? What happened? How did that new environment make you feel?*

- *The scripture above tells us that even when we walk in the darkest of places, God is close beside us. Have you ever felt God close when you were afraid?*

- *What is a situation you are nervous to face (for example, a new grade in school, a new job, a new sports team)? Does studying Psalm 23 change your nerves in any way? What is a practical way your family can help you with this new situation?*

Activity

Lead the Sheep: This is a game about listening for God's leading even when we're in the darkest valley. One family member is chosen to be "the sheep." Take that person out of the room, blindfold them, and then bring them back into the room. In the meantime, the other family members should put obstacles all around the room (turned-over chairs, toys, furniture, etc.). One family member will be the voice of the Lord and will give the blindfolded sheep verbal instructions on how to safely cross from one side of the room to the other without hitting any obstacles. While the sheep listens for the voice and tries to navigate the room, the other family members can be distractors by making noises and trying to confuse the sheep. Once the sheep safely makes it across, give everyone different roles and play again!

Thou Shalt Not Bear False Witness

Scripture

Colossians 3:9–10 NIV

⁹ *Do not lie to each other, since you have taken off your old self with its practices* ¹⁰ *and have put on the new self, which is being renewed in knowledge in the image of its Creator.*

Proverbs 10:9 ESV

⁹ *Whoever walks in integrity walks securely, but he who makes his ways crooked will be found out.*

Rainy with a Chance of Cell Phone (Madison)

Today's kids will never get to experience some of life's simplest pleasures: the sound of your dial-up internet starting, waking up in the middle of the night to take care of your Tamagotchi digital pet, and playing the game "Snake" on an early 2000s-era cell phone. That last one ended up teaching our brother Logan a very valuable lesson.

The year was 2001, and our family took a massive technological leap forward by investing in a family cell phone. Of course we had our trusty landline phone (kids, ask your parents about this), but this cell phone was going to bring us into the twenty-first century. It was a gold Nokia phone that looked and felt more like a brick than a current-day mobile phone, but even though it felt prehistoric, it contained the most important feature in the world to an elementary-aged boy: games. Being the youngest member of our family meant Logan was often out of luck when it came to access to the new family cell phone, but one memorable evening, his chance finally arrived.

Logan gripped the gold behemoth tightly in his hands and ran outside. Finally, he could take this new phone for a spin. He quickly found the phone's games, launched the "Snake" application, and for hours enjoyed zigging and zagging a very poorly animated, ever-growing snake around the screen eating equally poorly animated pellets. It was a great time to be alive and a nine-year-old boy. When Logan heard our mom's voice telling him to come in for dinner, he proudly trotted inside, eager to share his new high score in Snake with us. But in all his eagerness, Logan accidentally left the gold Nokia phone outside completely exposed to the elements. Phones back then were essentially indestructible, but that night the phone got put to the test as torrential rains poured down. Inside, Logan happily ate dinner, but outside, the poor family cell phone sat helpless in an onslaught of wind and rain. When the next morning finally came, the rains had subsided. And while he was enjoying his morning coffee, our dad asked Logan a question that sent a shockwave right through him. "Hey, where is the family cell phone?" It was in that moment that Logan realized his dire mistake. Memories of placing the gold Nokia on the ground and running inside for dinner played back in his mind. He had to act, and he had to act quickly.

Logan ran out to the place where he'd played with the family cell phone the evening prior, and lo and behold there it was shining like a golden nugget on the paved driveway. But upon further review, he noticed the phone was nearly submerged in pooled rainwater. His heart sank at the sight of it. Logan pulled the cell phone out of its bath and made a regretful decision ... he *was going to lie*. He gripped the phone and returned to our father. "Here it is! I forgot that I left the phone in the garage last night." To Logan this was brilliant; our dad would never know the truth. But when you're nine, details aren't your strong suit. Dad grabbed the moist cell phone and noticed almost instantly that something didn't add up with Logan's story. There was standing water on the buttons and moisture evident behind the screen. "Why is the phone dripping wet?" Dad asked. And with that one simple question, Logan's bogus story was busted immediately.

Thankfully, as mentioned, phones back then were indestructible. After a brief stint in a bag of uncooked white rice, all the moisture on the phone had dried and it was back to its former glory. Sadly, however, Logan found himself in hot water, more for lying to our dad than for forgetting the phone. His "Snake" playing days had come to an abrupt end, but Logan learned a valuable lesson that day. As the scripture from Proverbs says, when we walk in integrity, we experience true freedom. When we're honest, we can navigate life with confidence without any elaborate, made-up stories to keep straight. Lying will always create more of a mess than we ever intended ... and, ultimately, your parents will *always* figure it out.

Reflection Questions

- *Parents, tell your kids about a time you told a lie as a child. What happened? Did you get found out? What consequences did you face for lying?*

- *Have you ever been lied to? How did it make you feel to be the recipient of a lie?*

- *Today's scripture tells us when we come to relationship with Jesus that we take off our old self with its practices (including lying) and put on our new self, which is renewed in the image of God. What does it look like practically for you to take off your old self? How can your family help you stay in your new self with new practices?*

Activity

Snake: In honor of young Logan's phone faux pas, it's time to see what all the early 2000s fuss was about. Use a computer or laptop and visit snake.googlemaps.com for a modern-day version of the ancient cell phone game. You'll use the arrow keys on the computer to direct a train up, down, left, and right to intersect with and pick up train passengers. But you have to be careful not to run into any obstacles or bump into yourself. See who can get the highest score!

....

....

....

....

No Place Like Home

Scripture

Deuteronomy 4:9

⁹ *"Be careful never to forget what you yourself have seen. Do not let these memories escape from your mind as long as you live! And be sure to pass them on to your children and grandchildren."*

Proverbs 22:6 ESV

⁶ *Train up a child in the way he should go; even when he is old he will not depart from it.*

Too Fun to Leave (Taylor)

Raising teenagers is not for the faint of heart. This era of parenting ushers in new concerns that didn't exist when kids were younger: curfews, high school drama, first heartbreaks, first-time drivers, and the dreaded peer pressure. Our parents knew that though they raised us with the utmost care, even we would experience some of these common pitfalls that come with being a teenager. But to mitigate this risk and to do everything they could to help us not walk through the same struggles they had, Dad and Mom decided to get creative.

They determined the likelihood of us getting into unmanage-able trouble was really nonexistent if we were at home. And while they didn't want us to become total homebodies, they thought, *What if we can make our house the place the kids and all their friends wanted to spend their Friday nights? What if we made sure there was always something fun, but safe, happening at our house?* What began as a simple idea came to fruition, and it all started with the Mega Slip 'n Slide to end all Slip 'n Slides.

Word quickly spread about what was going down at the Cain house: a one-hundred-foot Slip 'n Slide of the magnitude no one had ever seen before. Mom and Dad had their work cut out for them and a quick turnaround to make it a reality. As they began their preparations, we began inviting our friends. As this tarp monstrosity took shape, our guest list grew into a monstrosity of its own. When the day of the event arrived, the Slip 'n Slide lay proudly in the backyard. It was a fifty-by-one-hundred-foot tarp masterpiece that started at the top of a slight hill and ended in the shallow waters of the pond behind our childhood home, sufficiently soaked with soapy water and doused with baby oil to increase the velocity of the sliders. It was perfect.

And then, carload by carload, a sea of youth descended upon our house. Before long there were nearly a hundred teenagers sprinting through the backyard and barreling into the pond. It was loud, it was messy, but it was incredible. On this evening, there was no drama to contend with, no threat of underage drinking or drugs. There was just pure, wholesome fun.

When we had slipped and slid to our hearts' content, we all came inside to play cards and watch movies deep into the night. As our friends finally left the house, they all raved about the fun they had and couldn't wait to see what our parents would come up with next! While the thought of whipping together another epic activity felt a tad ominous to Mom and Dad, they knew their plan had worked. They had made our home the epicenter of fun, offering a wholesome alternative to the things the world had to offer. A teen could spend Friday and Saturday nights at our house and rest assured they wouldn't be tempted to get into trouble or make a life-defining mistake. We could all just have fun, and we could glorify God in the process.

This trend held strong throughout our high school. Even as we moved into our college years and early adulthood, we continued to bring friends home most weekends. As the scripture above says, train up a child in the way they should go and even when they are old, they won't depart from it. This truth most certainly came to pass for our parents. They trained us in the way of God-honoring, wholesome memory-making and, to this day, we have yet to depart from it.

Reflection Questions

- *Parents, share about a time you got yourself into some trouble as a teenager. What happened? What do you wish you would have done differently?*
- *Go around the table and answer this question: What is your most fun memory that you've shared as a family?*
- *The scripture says to train up a child in the way they should go. Parents, share with your kids some things you are hoping to train them up in. What are some of the good things you are praying for their lives?*

Activity

It's time to plan a Friday Fun Night of your own! Look ahead at the calendar and schedule this night of fun. What would your family enjoy doing? Making a Slip 'n Slide? Going to an arcade? Going to dinner and a movie? Whatever your family enjoys together, set aside an upcoming Friday and have fun! While you're at it, consider inviting others to join in the fun, just as our parents welcomed those energetic teenagers to our house and created lifelong memories.

....
....
....
....
....
....
....
....
....
....
....
....
....
....

No Greater Love

Scripture
John 15:12–13

[12] *"This is my commandment: Love each other in the same way I have loved you. [13] There is no greater love than to lay down one's life for one's friends."*

Dashing through the Snow (Taylor)

The great state of Alabama is known for many things, but one thing most certainly *not* on that list is snow. So, on the rarest of occasions, when the cool air from the Appalachian and Rocky Mountain ranges converges on the heart of the Southeast, snow falls in Alabama and the entire state loses its mind. Schools close immediately, local grocery stores have their milk and bread supply vanish into thin air, and, most importantly, residents get outside and play! Our family was no different. At the first sight of snow on the ground, our entire family would bundle up and spend our day playing in the wintry sludge that is Alabama snow. But one fateful snow day our family's fun and games took a terrifying turn.

Our family and some dear friends decided to join together for an epic adventure. Together we built small, misshapen snowmen, we waged war with snowballs, and lastly we decided to use the frozen streets for some intense laundry basket sledding. The streets were all vacant due to the icy conditions, so they were a sledder's dream. Our dad loaded us into simple, plastic laundry baskets and gave us a hearty shove along the frozen street. We all squealed with delight as we zoomed along the ice before coming to a gentle stop on the powdery snowbank located at the street's dead end. This created an unending cycle of sled pushing for our dad as we would immediately run back to the top of the street for him to give us another launch.

After what had to have felt like push number one thousand for the afternoon, we decided to go inside for a break from the cold. But in typical young-boy fashion, two of our friends stayed behind to set out on their own for one final sled. The boys got a significant running start and jumped into their laundry basket. Right away it was clear this would be the fastest slide of the day. The basket blistered down the abandoned street and barreled toward the powdery snowbank. But on this slide, the boys had gained too much speed to be stopped. They hit the snowbank, continued through a line of thick trees, and flew off the edge of a fifteen-foot cliff. As the boys disappeared through trees our family and friends all ran in their direction. No one was aware of this surprise drop-off until they heard the boys yelling for help.

Panic instantly washed over the adults as they heard the cries and pushed through the thick tree line. Thankfully, their worst nightmares were alleviated when they discovered neither of the boys was injured. But they still were in quite the predicament; the ground surrounding the cliff was as slick as the frozen street, and try as they might, the boys could not climb to safety. It appeared they were trapped at the bottom of this icy cliff that formed a sort of pit. Our dad, brimming with adrenaline, had been the first on the scene. Dad did everything he could to safely retrieve them. That was until he, too, slipped on the icy ground and found himself joining the boys at the bottom of the cliff. What followed was a perfect case in point for the definition of insanity, which is "doing the same thing over and over and expecting different results." One by one, the adults in our convoy would try their luck at safely descending the cliff to pull the boys (and now our dad) to safety, and one by one the adults would inevitably lose their footing and slide down the cliff on their backsides. Even young Logan tried to be a hero at merely six years old, and it went about as poorly as you'd imagine; he wound up at the bottom of the cliff too.

There were now *seven* people huddled together at the base of the cliff. They tried various strategies, but each one ended with them in the same place—*stranded.* The only people wise enough to not try their luck with the cliff were Madison and me. After watching our family and friends fall to their icy fate, we hatched a novel idea: go get help. We dashed to a nearby neighbor's house, used the phone to call 911, and quickly a local ambulance and first responder team was on the scene. With the proper ladders and other tools from their emergency vehicle, the team was able to pull each person up from the bottom one by one until they were all safely together again.

While our respective rescue efforts had been unsuccessful (apart from those of the trained rescue personnel), everyone's willingness to put their own safety and comfort at risk to help one another was a beautiful display of the love of Jesus. While teaching His disciples, Jesus gave His followers a new commandment: to love one another in the same way that He loved them. And above all else, Jesus' love was selfless and sacrificial. He put *His* safety and comfort by the wayside and laid down His life for us in the most powerful act of love the world would ever know, and He's called us to go and do likewise.

We all hugged each other tightly as we gave our sincere thanks to the first responders and turned to journey back home. Glory to God, we all walked away uninjured to enjoy some nice hot cocoa and to promptly put away our death-trap, laundry basket sleds for good.

Reflections Questions:

- *Parents, share with your kids about a time you did something risky growing up like the boys from the story. What happened? Did you end up getting hurt or getting into trouble?*
- *Today's scripture says that we are to love one another as Christ Jesus has loved us. What are the ways He has loved you? What does it look like for us to love one another in that same way?*
- *The passage ends with Jesus saying, "There is no greater love than to lay down one's life for one's friends." In our story, the adults were willing to risk their physical safety to help their stranded friends.. But what does Jesus mean here? How do we "lay down our lives" for our friends? What does that mean to you?*

Activity

Indoor Snowball Fight: In honor of the snow day story, today you're going to play an indoor game that is fun year-round. All you'll need is roughly fifty pieces of scratch paper. Work together to crumple each piece into a "snowball" about the size of the palm of your hand. Place all the snowballs into a pile in the center of the living room. Then divide the family into two teams. Teams will be placed on either side of the room with the pile of snowballs midway between them. The goal is to throw as many snowballs as possible onto the other team's side of the room in two minutes. Once two minutes is up, stop and count the snowballs on each side of the room. The team with the lower number of snowballs on their side wins!

The Faith of a Child

Scripture

Matthew 18:2-4 ESV

[2] *And calling to him a child, he put him in the midst of them* [3] *and said, "Truly, I say to you, unless you turn and become like children, you will never enter the kingdom of heaven.* [4] *Whoever humbles himself like this child is the greatest in the kingdom of heaven."*

Mark 10:14-15 ESV

[14] *But when Jesus saw it, he was indignant and said to them, "Let the children come to me; do not hinder them, for to such belongs the kingdom of God.* [15] *Truly, I say to you, whoever does not receive the kingdom of God like a child shall not enter it."*

Appen-Deck the Halls (Taylor)

Christmas at the Cain family house has always been the most warm and magical time of the year, and no Christmas is more memorable in our eyes than the Christmas of 1998. But if you asked our parents, their take on this particular time would be vastly different. On December 23, our family made the trek north into Tennessee to enjoy an extended family gathering before Christmas at Nana's house. We were all brimming with excitement. We were excited to play with our cousins and visit with our grandmother, sure, but what we were most excited about was the fact that in about thirty-six hours, the one and only Santa Claus would make his way to our Alabama home to deliver a bevy of presents. Our childlike wonder had us sitting in the back seat of the family car staring out the window and envisioning the jolly old man in red shimmying down our chimney with his sack of toys. Our daydreaming was so enthralling that we failed to notice the warning signs that our mom, Shari, wasn't feeling so well.

Throughout the family gathering, Mom was experiencing significant pain in her stomach. It started as a dull ache, but as the day went on, it became more of a sharp, intense pain. She tried her best to tough it out and keep her Christmas spirit, but by the time the family function was over she was quite miserable. We had plans to stay the night with family friends in a nearby Tennessee town, so following the party, we made our way there with Mom becoming more and more ill throughout the journey. By the time we arrived, it was evident that Mom couldn't stay for a visit; she needed to be taken to the emergency room as quickly as possible to see about this acute abdominal pain. Dad dropped us three off with our friends and sped Mom to the closest ER. Thank the Lord for quick thinking, because shortly after they arrived at the hospital, the source of our mom's pain was found to be none other than a ruptured appendix. She had to be rushed to surgery right away to have what was left of her appendix removed before it could do any more damage to her body. As she was wheeled to the operating room in the early morning hours of Christmas Eve, she couldn't help but think of what we were feeling.

Back at our family friends' house, we were in knots. Of course, we were concerned about our mother and longing to have her well, but at the ages of six and eight, we couldn't keep from being nervous about the Christmas implications. "Tonight's going to be Christmas Eve. What if we end up having to stay here in Tennessee tonight? Will Santa even know where we are?" a young, analytical Madison pondered aloud. She'd always tried her hardest to stay up late to catch St. Nick in action, but if there was ever a time to doubt, it was this one.

While mom began to recover from a successful appendectomy, we were sequestered far from home, out of state, and there was no way in our minds that Santa would be able to course correct this late in the game. But even in the extenuating circumstances, we clung to even the slightest sliver of hope that Santa would know exactly what to do. Christmas Eve day turned into Christmas Eve night, and thankfully by this time we were aware that our mother was recovering beautifully and would be able to leave the hospital the next day. But this also meant we would in fact be spending the night before Christmas away from home.

Little Madison sat at the top of the unfamiliar stairs late into the night. She couldn't sleep, so she thought she would take the first Santa Watch. As the minutes turned into hours, her hopes dwindled. Finally, she relented, curled up into a blanket, and slept there at the top of the stairs—until she heard her brother's voice.

"Madison, Madison, wake up! You won't believe this," Logan exclaimed. Madison roused from her blanket and followed him. "He came, he came! Santa found us here," Logan continued, at this point bouncing with every word. The pair grabbed me out of bed, and we raced downstairs. When we made it to the bottom step, Logan's excitement was confirmed. There, nestled under the Christmas tree, were three sets of Christmas gifts. Somehow, some way, Santa Claus had heard about our predicament and managed to find us in this unfamiliar territory.

As we tore into our presents, our parents returned from the hospital with Mom feeling considerably better and so thankful to be back with us. While we could hardly wait to show our mom and dad how Santa had pulled off a Christmas miracle, our parents couldn't help but smile watching our childlike faith shine brightly. Right away, we believed with our whole hearts that Santa had done the unthinkable. This type of wholehearted, sold-out belief was ultimately what Jesus was getting at when He challenged His followers to become like children. A *childlike* faith is not one that is child*ish*, but is a faith built on complete trust in Jesus. And this complete trust is how we are to receive the kingdom of God.

Reflection Questions

- *In the scripture passages above, Jesus encourages his disciples to receive the kingdom of God like a child. What does that mean to you? How does a child receive a gift?*
- *Jesus also said whoever humbles himself like a child shall be greatest in the kingdom of heaven. Is that surprising to you? What does it look like practically to humble oneself like a child?*
- *What are some practices your family can do to ensure you all have pure faith like that of children?*

The Feather Game: All you'll need is a single feather and a timer. The object of the game is to have a person keep the feather in the air for as long as possible using only their breath. Whoever keeps the feather in the air the longest wins!

The point of the game is simple—what keeps the feather in the air? The breath! But we can't see the breath, so how do we know it's lifting the feather? There's lots of evidence—we see the person's lips moving, we hear their breathing, we see the effects on the feather, etc. This can be related to our faith in God. While we can't see God, we can have faith that He is real because we see evidence of His presence all around us. We feel His peace in our lives, we feel His comfort in difficult times—what other evidence in your lives proves God is real?

....

....

....

....

....

....

....

....

....

....

Forgiveness

Scripture

Colossians 3:12–15

[12] *Since God chose you to be the holy people he loves, you must clothe yourselves with tenderhearted mercy, kindness, humility, gentleness, and patience.* [13] *Make allowance for each other's faults, and forgive anyone who offends you. Remember, the Lord forgave you, so you must forgive others.* [14] *Above all, clothe yourselves with love, which binds us all together in perfect harmony.* [15] *And let the peace that comes from Christ rule in your hearts. For as members of one body you are called to live in peace.*

A Family Restored (Madison)

Growing up, our mom, Shari, knew her family situation was *unique*, to say the least. Just before she was born, her biological father decided to leave her mother and older sister. He didn't go very far, however. He just moved to a different town nearby and sunk himself deep into his work. His mind was too busy and his work schedule too full to concern himself with a family, so he made this decision that altered more lives than just his own.

Into her early childhood years, Mom would recall her father driving by her home on rare occasions. He would drop off money to help with the bills or for groceries, but the monetary gifts were no real substitute for dropping by to say hello and spend time with his daughters. Nana would go on to remarry a wonderful man who treated Mom and her sister as if they were his own, but there was still a part of Mom that longed for a relationship with her mysterious, transient, biological father. She had all sorts of questions. "Why did he leave us? Did he have any interest in knowing me or my sister? How could he do this to us?" Mom did her best to put this longing out of her mind because she feared that a relationship with him would never be possible. And for decades, this fear proved to be true, until Nana heard a very surprising word from the Lord.

Mom had grown into a wife and mother of three herself, and she was fulfilled with her thriving life with her own family. So she was a bit taken aback when Nana came to her with an unexpected message. "I feel like God is telling me that I need to set up a meeting with your father, and I need to tell him that I forgive him," Nana stated confidently. Mom was shocked to hear these words, but she was even more shocked when Nana requested that Mom and her sister join in on this meeting. Mom reluctantly agreed, but leading up to the meeting she was a nervous wreck. What would she say? How would he respond? Would he get angry?

All these questions swirled in her mind as she walked slowly with Nana and her sister to this profound meeting. And then, at once, there he was seated before them. Nana started the meeting with the simple and powerful word that the Lord had given her. "I wanted to have this meeting to look you in the eyes and tell you that I forgive you for leaving us," Nana said sincerely. Instantly, that display of unmerited grace washed over her father. His reaction was not defensive nor angry but overwhelmed with thankfulness. His eyes filled with tears, and, through shaky words, he thanked Nana for her kindness. He asked his daughters for forgiveness that he knew he didn't deserve, and he shared his hopes to make up for lost time and start a relationship with them.

Mom wasn't prepared for this response. She certainly wasn't expecting a request to rekindle a relationship after all these years. But in the same way that the word from the Lord had stirred Nana, this request stirred our mom. She forgave her father in that moment and accepted his request to start a relationship with him. Her father rose from his chair and the two shared a long-overdue hug. What the Enemy had hoped to use for evil and destruction, the Lord was turning into good in that very moment.

Over twenty years have gone by since that historic day. And glory to God, Mom's relationship with her father is healthy, present, and thriving. He is a permanent fixture in all our lives to the degree that we take a yearly family beach vacation together. The Lord challenges us to forgive others as He forgave us, and in this instance, that forgiveness was the key to a loving father-daughter relationship that has far exceeded the hurt caused by past mistakes.

Reflection Questions

- *The scripture above tells us to clothe ourselves in tender-hearted mercy, kindness, humility, gentleness, and patience. Which of these come most naturally to you? Which one is the most difficult for you to clothe yourself in?*
- *Forgiving someone who has wronged you can be so diffi-cult. Yet the Lord tells us in this scripture that in light of*

how we've been forgiven by God for all our sin, we are to forgive other people. Is there someone in your life you need to forgive? If you aren't ready to take that step, talk about it with your family and pray for God to show you how you should approach the situation.

- *The scripture also says that clothing ourselves in love binds us together in perfect harmony. How can we practically clothe ourselves in love?*

Activity

Tonight clothe yourselves in love toward each other—it's Family Night! Work together to decide what is for dinner and all pitch in with the cooking. Then, after dinner, pick out a favorite movie for you all to enjoy together! No phones, no other screens, just time together! Enjoy!

....

....

....

....

....

....

....

....

....

God's Timing

Scripture

Jeremiah 29:11

[11] *"For I know the plans I have for you," says the Lord. "They are plans for good and not for disaster, to give you a future and a hope."*

Psalm 27:13–14

[13] *Yet I am confident I will see the Lord's goodness while I am here in the land of the living.* [14] *Wait patiently for the Lord. Be brave and courageous. Yes, wait patiently for the Lord.*

Our Year (Madison)

After six years of pursuing music as a career, it seemed like we had finally "made it." We signed our first record deal, and *this* was going to be CAIN's year! We recorded our first six songs and landed our very first music tour with the legendary Zach Williams and We The Kingdom. Before we even had a song on Christian music radio, our calendar filled up with eighty booked concerts. After so many years of struggling to make music and survive, it appeared that everything was finally going our way. We could hardly believe it, but we *knew* this was *our* year. What we didn't anticipate is what else was on the way in this, our year: 2020.

Let's rewind and pretend we don't know what's about to go down in that unprecedented year. Imagine you're with us in Clearwater, Florida, for the opening night of the Zach Williams Rescue Story Tour. CAIN is trying out our matching baby blue outfits for the first time on a live audience. (Who told me that wearing baby blue fur was a good idea for southern Florida?) Soaked in sweat and anxiety, we take the stage. I'm so nervous that my arms go numb. Taylor's voice is a little shaky, but we're doing it. We'd had the brilliant idea to give away a CAIN T-shirt during our short fifteen-minute music set. So Logan tries to throw the shirt to a lucky fan, but it unfolds and hits the air like a weak sail. Rather than soaring into the crowd, it only manages to land about two feet in front of our microphone stands.

We play our freshly recorded songs "Rise Up," "The Commission," and "Yes He Can." At the end of our set, to our surprise, we receive a standing ovation. We are elated, relieved, and so hopeful for the rest of the year. This first weekend of touring has been the best time of our lives. What could possibly go wrong?

We didn't know, of course, that a mere five days later a coronavirus pandemic would cancel the tour along with the rest of our eighty booked shows for 2020. Our calendar, once full, was now empty. We had no clue our debut single "Rise Up" would flatline on the Christian radio charts and struggle to be played across the country. Our hopes for our music, once high, were now brought to their lowest point. In the blink of an eye, it looked as if "our year" would go down as yet another failed attempt at a music career.

What followed, however, was the most valuable lesson we could ever receive as Christian music artists or even as Christ followers in general. Things didn't magically improve a few weeks into the pandemic; it took a full calendar year before some normalcy returned to the music industry. But it was in this time of quiet, this time of uncertainty, that we got to see firsthand that our dreams, our music, our calling—none of these things were under *our* control nor adhered to *our* timing. God had opened doors and made a way for us to even get to this point. Yet at the sight of this seemingly insurmountable obstacle, we feared, we doubted, and we tried to grip tightly to our career. We couldn't tour, we couldn't meet with radio stations across the country to promote our song, and we couldn't even get together with people to write music. We felt ourselves slipping into an emotional pit, saying, "It wasn't supposed to be this way."

But then, it was as if the Lord pulled us up out of the mire. We met together, just us three, and resolved among ourselves, "Okay, we may not be able to do the things we had planned to do, but we *can* do something." We started to pray and brainstorm, and the Lord kept depositing ideas into our minds. We decided we would live stream ourselves and play music online once per week. We agreed to handwrite letters to every Christian radio station across the country in lieu of an in-person visit. And we settled that we would take this opportunity to write more music together and practice as much as we could. For the months that followed, we remained faithful to this plan. At points it felt futile, but each moment we'd become discouraged, the Lord would remind us of what we'd resolved to do. It was as if along the way, when we would grow weary, He would put his arm around our shoulders and say, "Stay strong, I have something in store for you." Then the miraculous happened.

Like a locomotive slowly gaining steam, our first song "Rise Up" began playing on more and more radio stations. It took on a life that we could have never anticipated. The Lord was speaking to people across the country, encouraging them that they, like Lazarus, could rise from their own grave of sin, shame, and circumstances. We were blown away hearing real-life stories of people sick in the hospital with COVID struggling to breathe finding strength and declaring over themselves, "Take a breath, you're alive now." God showed us that our music, our callings, would never be about *us*. He didn't need us to tour or promote or put together a perfectly planned calendar. He just needed us to be faithful to write the songs He'd given us, and He would be the one in charge of getting those songs to the people who needed to hear them the most.

Thankfully, the nerve-wracking year that was 2020 came to a close, and we began to return to normal the following year. But we treasured the lessons we learned in that time. Our plan wouldn't be the one that would have the impact on the world. It always was and always will be *God's* plan. If we are brave and courageous to patiently wait on the Lord, as the psalm says, we will see His goodness in our lives.

Reflection Questions

- *What was the most difficult aspect of the pandemic for you? Were there any parts of that time that you enjoyed? Did your family get any extended time together?*

- *The scripture above states that the Lord has good plans for us and our lives. Have you ever had trouble believing that?*
- *God's Word also says to be brave and courageous and wait on the Lord. What does it mean to you to "wait" on the Lord? What are some practical ways we can wait for the Lord and trust in His plan and His timing?*

Activity

Gratitude Check: At times when we don't immediately understand what God is planning for our lives, it's good to stop, reflect, give thanks for all He has already done, and remember His faithfulness and goodness. If He's been faithful before, He will undoubtedly be faithful again. As a family, make a Gratitude List. Write down your name and something for which you are thankful, or a prayer that was answered and the date it occurred. Keep this Gratitude List on your refrigerator or another place where your family can easily see it each day. Remember, God is a God who is in the details, so nothing is too small or insignificant to be grateful for!

....

....

....

....

....

....

Acknowledgments

Setting out to write a forty-day devotional was certainly no small feat, and so, as with everything in our family, it took a village!

First and foremost, we want to thank our Lord and Savior Jesus Christ. You are the reason we sing, and we hope only to bring you glory.

Second, we want to thank our incredible and selfless spouses and our inspiring children. Being your family is an honor like no other.

Mom and Dad, there is no book without you. Thank you for looking like Jesus whether you were in the pulpit on a Sunday morning or at home on a Monday afternoon. Your fingerprints are on every one of these stories, and we hope you know how massive your impact has been not only on us, but on the entire world. We love you.

Ron, there are plenty of good managers out there, but you are truly *great* management. We love you and thank you for believing in us to reach higher and push further.

Thank you to our amazing team at KLOVE Books for believing in this project and for making this devotional come to life. A special thank you to Karen and Rebekah for your thoughtful feedback and tireless work!

About the Authors

The music of CAIN quickly became a mainstay at radio since their debut single, the RIAA Gold® certified "Rise Up (Lazarus)," was released in early 2020. In addition to "Rise Up (Lazarus)" their single "I'm So Blessed" has also recently received RIAA Gold® certification. Raised in Hartselle, Alabama as pastor's kids and now residing in Nashville, CAIN - Madison Cain Johnson, Taylor Cain Matz, and Logan Cain - got their first break opening for Dave Barnes at a show in 2012. Now more than a decade later, they've headlined their own tour, along with sharing the stage with Christian music's best like Chris Tomlin, Zach Williams, Casting Crowns, TobyMac, and even performed on the Grand Ole Opry stage. The group also hosted the 2023 K-LOVE Fan Awards.

They've hit No. 1 back-to-back at radio with their first two singles, "Rise Up (Lazarus)" and "Yes He Can," both songs from their first full-length album Rise Up. Additionally, their viral single "I'm So Blessed" took over the streaming front, amassing more than 56M streams to date worldwide. Because of its social media popularity, more than 200,000 people have created their own videos using the music of "I'm So Blessed," accounting for 400M additional views on social media and growing their social media reach by 185%. This song has been both the inspiration for a new children's book, I'm So Blessed, written by the band and released in August 2024, as well as the family devotional, We're So Blessed: A 40-Day Guide to Gratefulness for the Whole Family.

In their career to date they've won a K-LOVE Fan Award for Top Breakout Single for "Rise Up (Lazarus)" and other recent nominations include Artist of the Year, Group of the Year, TV/Streaming Impact, various other KLOVE awards, numerous Dove Awards, and an American Music Award (AMA). They recently released their very own television show on TBN called, Chasing CAIN, which highlights the realities of life as a touring family. The series received rave reviews and even garnered the 2024 Dove Award for "Television Series of the Year." Their latest musical release, Jesus Music (Deluxe), is out now on all streaming platforms.

Apart from their multi-faceted work, CAIN finds their most enjoyment spending time at home in Nashville, TN with their families. Each member of CAIN and their spouses welcomed their first children into the world in 2022 and have since continued growing their families even more with Logan having his second child in the fall of 2023 and both Taylor and Madison welcoming second babies in the fall of 2024 and spring of 2025 respectively.

It has been said that if you spend five minutes with the members of CAIN, you'll feel like you've spent the afternoon in the sunshine. Their joy spills over onto each person they meet, their bright smiles as contagious as their stunning harmonies. Pouring their joy into their music, CAIN has discovered what it's like to live their calling while doing their favorite thing - singing about Jesus.

BOOKS
THAT
INSPIRE

FROM THE
ARTISTS
YOU LOVE

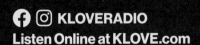